America's Most Notorious Domestic Terrorists: The Life and Crimes of the Unabomber and Timothy McVeigh

By Charles River Editors

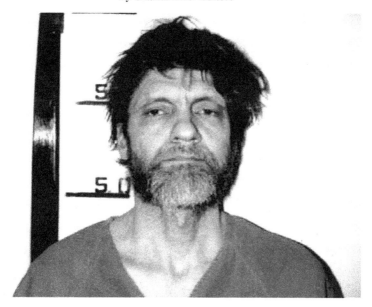

Kaczynski's mugshot

Introduction

The Unabomber

The sketch used for the Unabomber before his capture

"But what first motivated me wasn't anything I read. I just got mad seeing the machines ripping up the woods and so forth..." – Ted Kaczynski

Most Americans old enough to follow the news during the 1990s are instantly familiar with the Unabomber, a name given to the man behind a series of bombs that were periodically mailed or delivered to university professors and airlines, which led to the FBI giving the investigation the codename "UNABOM," an acronym for "University and Airline Bomber." Over nearly 20 years, the Unabomber, as he was dubbed by the media, would kill 3 and wound dozens with his homemade bombs, some of which were primitive but others of which were strong enough to destroy an airplane.

While authorities struggled to find him from the first time he targeted someone with a bomb in 1978, the Unabomber 's choice of targets and the materials he used offered a glimpse into the kind of man he was. Profilers rightly assumed that it was a man who had received a higher education and had some sort of interest in the environment and big business. What they could not know at the time was that it was all the work of one man, Ted Kaczynski, who was the product of a Harvard education and had briefly taught at UCLA before retiring to a cabin in Montana without electricity or running water.

Ultimately, it was Kaczynski who tripped himself up thanks to his insistence that a major media outlet publish his lengthy essay *Industrial Society and Its Future*. Now known almost universally as the Unabomber Manifesto, it was a long screed against the effects of industry and technology on nature, and the way technology has impacted the psychology and personalities of people in society. Often incorporating "FC" in his bombs and writings as shorthand for Freedom Club, Kaczynski also asserted that the dependence on technology limited people's freedom and sapped them of their desire for personal autonomy.

Eventually, federal authorities rightly figured that publication of the Manifesto might actually lead to someone recognizing the author, and it was Ted's younger brother, David, who led investigators to Ted. While thousands of people sent misleading clues in the wake of the Manifesto being published, David worked discreetly to try to collect evidence that might suggest Ted's guilt before tipping off the FBI. A search warrant that allowed a raid on Ted's cabin in Montana on April 3, 1996 made clear that the Feds had found their man, and after Kaczynski refused to plead insane, he was eventually given a life sentence without the possibility of parole after a guilty plea.

Timothy McVeigh

The Alfred P. Murrah Building before McVeigh's attack

"Think about the people as if they were storm troopers in Star Wars. They may be individually innocent, but they are guilty because they work for the Evil Empire." – Timothy McVeigh

Two days after Ramzi Yousef's attack on the World Trade Center in 1993, federal agents from the Bureau of Alcohol, Tobacco and Firearms (ATF), the FBI and the Texas National Guard surrounded the Mount Carmel Center compound outside of Waco, Texas. They were there to search the property of the Branch Davidians, a religious cult, due to allegations that cult members were sexually abusing children and had assault weapons. When they began searching, the Branch Davidians, led by David Koresh, fired on them, starting a firefight and a nearly two month long siege of the compound.

The siege of the compound ended on April 19, 1993 with the deaths of over 75 cult members, including children, and in the wake of the event there was a lot of soul searching, but in addition to influencing how the government approached potential future conflicts with other groups, Waco's most important legacy was that it enraged people who already had an anti-government bent. As it turned out, the most notable was a young Gulf War veteran named Timothy McVeigh, who came to Waco during the siege and shouted his support for gun rights.

After the siege ended, McVeigh was determined to strike back at the federal government. In 1994, McVeigh and an old Army buddy, Michael Fortier, decided they would bomb the Alfred P. Murrah Federal Building in Oklahoma City because several federal agencies had offices inside, including the ATF. With the help of Terry Nichols, McVeigh constructed a bomb out of fertilizer that weighed over two tons and placed it in a rented Ryder truck, the same company Ramzi Yousef had rented a van from.

At 9:00 a.m. on April 19, 1995, the second anniversary of the end of the siege in Waco, McVeigh's bomb exploded with a force so powerful that it registered seismic readings across much of Oklahoma and could be heard 50 miles away. The explosion killed 168 people, including young children in the building's day-care center. McVeigh was captured shortly after the explosion, and he never displayed remorse for his actions. When he later learned about the day-care center, McVeigh called the children "collateral damage."

At the time, the bombing was the deadliest terrorist attack on American soil in history, and McVeigh was executed on June 11, 2001, three months before the bombing became the second deadliest terrorist attack on American soil in history.

America's Most Notorious Domestic Terrorists: The Life and Crimes of the Unabomber and Timothy McVeigh chronicle the stories of two of the most famous domestic terrorists of the 20th century. Along with pictures of important people, places, and events, you will learn about the Unabomber and Timothy McVeigh like never before.

America's Most Notorious Domestic Terrorists: The Life and Crimes of the Unabomber and Timothy McVeigh

The Unabomber

A Force That Is Too Powerful

"There is no contradiction here; an individual whose attitudes or behavior bring him into conflict with the system is up against a force that is too powerful for him to conquer or escape from, hence he is likely to suffer from stress, frustration, defeat. His path will be much easier if he thinks and behaves as the system requires. In that sense the system is acting for the benefit of the individual when it brainwashes him into conformity." – Excerpt from the Unabomber's Manifesto

In many ways, it seems that Ted Kaczynski never really stood a chance for normal development. Born on May 22, 1942 in Evergreen Park, Illinois, his parents, Theodore and Wanda Kaczynski, were Polish Americans during a time of rising xenophobia, exposing them and their son to all sorts of unwanted comments. Then, there was the matter of his health; while still an infant, he developed a severe case of hives that doctors treated by periodically isolating him in a hospital room, away from all non-medical human contact.

It is impossible to tell the what if any long-term damage was done by these repeated hospitalizations, but at one point his mother observed that his was "quite unresponsive after his experience," and in her psychological evaluation of Kaczynski, Dr. Sally C. Johnson's noted, "Conflicting reports exist as to the significance of that hospitalization. Records reviewed through notes kept in Mr. Kaczynski's baby book do not provide much information in regard to problems following that hospitalization. Information provided by Wanda Kaczynski, however, indicates her perception that his hospitalization was a significant and traumatic event for her son, in that he experienced a separation from his mother (due to routine hospital practices). She describes him as having changed after the hospitalization in that he was withdrawn, less responsive, and more fearful of separation from her after that point in time. …somewhat conflicting accounts exist as to his early social development. He was viewed as a bright child and was described by his mother as not being particularly comfortable around other children and displaying fears of people and buildings. She noted that he played beside other children rather than with them. Her concern about him apparently led her to consider enrolling him in a study being conducted by Bruno Betleheim regarding autistic children."

In spite of his early trauma, it seems that Kaczynski still enjoyed a relatively peaceful childhood until he was 7 years old, when he suddenly lost his "only child" status with the birth of his younger brother, David. Kaczynski's aunt later recalled, "Before David was born, Teddy was different. When they'd visit, he'd snuggle up to me. Then, when David was born, something must have happened. He changed immediately. Maybe we paid too much attention to the new baby." His parents became concerned when he withdrew into himself repeatedly, neither speaking to nor interacting with other was varying periods of time. However, as an adult Kaczynski himself did not see this as a problem, as Dr. Johnson pointed out: "Mr. Kaczynski describes his early childhood as relatively uneventful, until the age of eight or nine. He described memories of early play with other children, although he too recounts being somewhat fearful of people and describes himself as socially reserved. He recounts a few significant episodes in his early life referencing the hospitalization mentioned above.... He does specifically describe extreme verbal and emotional abuse during his upbringing, although he did not identify this as a problem until he was in his 20s. ... He remembers his mother focusing on his dialect, encouraging him not to talk like the kids in the street, and responds that he complied by speaking one way at home and another way when interacting with the other children. By the age of eight or nine, Mr. Kaczynski describes that he was no longer well accepted by the neighborhood children or his peers at school. The neighborhood children "bordered on delinquency" by his account, and he was not willing or interested in being involved in their activities. The family moved several times, bettering their housing status, eventually moving to Evergreen Park, Illinois, when he was approximately age 10. He describes this as a middle class suburb of Chicago."

Their new home seemed idyllic by all appearances, and Kaczynski's parents threw themselves into giving their children the best of the American dream, most especially academically. Dr. Roy Weinberg, who lived near them during this period, later called them "a serious family" and added, "They read books all the time. ... [Ted] was strictly a loner. This kid didn't play. No. No. He was an old man before his time. ... Both boys were more interested in books than sports, but the younger brother seemed to have friends, while his older brother was a loner. They were completely different, night and day."

The perfect storm that seemed to be determined to shape Kaczynski into a social misfit continued into his elementary school years. When he was in 5th grade, his IQ was tested and judged to be 167, and as a result of this information, the school district had him skip the 6th grade and go on into the 7th. This proved to be a disaster from a social standpoint because he did not fit in at all with the older students. He was bullied, teased and isolated from most of the school's social groups, and he began to develop phobias about being in strange places or around people he did not know. According to Johnson, "Mr. Kaczynski described this skipping a grade as a pivotal event in his life. He remembers not fitting in with the older children and being the subject of considerable verbal abuse and teasing from them. He did not describe having any close friends during that period of time."

For his part, Kaczynski seems to have remained bitter about the way in which the school system treated him. He wrote in his notorious Manifesto, "Education is no longer a simple affair of paddling a kid's behind when he doesn't know his lessons and patting him on the head when he does know them. It is becoming a scientific technique for controlling the child's development. Sylvan Learning Centers, for example, have had great success in motivating children to study, and psychological techniques are also used with more or less success in many conventional schools. 'Parenting' techniques that are taught to parents are designed to make children accept fundamental values of the system and behave in ways that the system finds desirable. 'Mental health' programs, 'intervention' techniques, psychotherapy and so forth are ostensibly designed to benefit individuals, but in practice they usually serve as methods for inducing individuals to think and behave as the system requires."

As is often the case with the intellectually gifted, Kaczynski found a respite from his isolation during high school, when he was freer to pursue his intellectual preferences. Classmate Bill Phelan recalled that Ted " was reading books, and I was playing sports and drinking beer. He wasn't in my world. He was in his own world." But Kaczynski did form a few tenuous relationships with other students, a group the *New York Times* subsequently described as "chess players with Elvis pompadours, teen-age pipe smokers marveling at Isaac Asimov and Ray Bradbury and fantasizing about landing on the moon." One of these young men, Patrick Morris, later said, "Ted was technically very bright, but emotionally deficient. While the math club would sit around talking about the big issues of the day, Ted would be waiting for someone to fart. He had a fascination with body sounds more akin to a 5-year-old than a 15-year-old." Morris further added that, during one intense discussion, "Ted seemed more interested in smearing cake frosting on this guy's nose." Russel Mosny may have been Kaczynski's closest friend at that time and described him as "the smartest kid in the class. He was just quiet and shy until you got to know him. Once he knew you, he could talk and talk. ... I'd try to get him to go to the sock hops, but he always said he'd rather play chess or read a book."

Looking back at Ted's high school years, Dr. Johnson observed, "He attended high school at Evergreen Park Community High School. He did well overall from an academic standpoint but reports some difficulty with math in his sophomore year. He was subsequently placed in a more advanced math class and mastered the material, then skipped the 11th grade. As the result, he completed his high school education two years early, although this did require him to take a summer school course in English. During the latter years of high school he was encouraged to apply to Harvard, and was subsequently accepted as a student, beginning in the fall of 1958. He was 16 years old at the time."

Mosny always considered this part of Kaczynski's problem: "They packed him up and sent him to Harvard before he was ready. He didn't even have a driver's license."

Oversocialization

"26. Oversocialization can lead to low self-esteem, a sense of powerlessness, defeatism, guilt, etc. One of the most important means by which our society socializes children is by making them feel ashamed of behavior or speech that is contrary to society's expectations. If this is overdone, or if a particular child is especially susceptible to such feelings, he ends by feeling ashamed of HIMSELF. Moreover the thought and the behavior of the oversocialized person are more restricted by society's expectations than are those of the lightly socialized person. The majority of people engage in a significant amount of naughty behavior. They lie, they commit petty thefts, they break traffic laws, they goof off at work, they hate someone, they say spiteful things or they use some underhanded trick to get ahead of the other guy. The oversocialized person cannot do these things, or if he does do them he generates in himself a sense of shame and self-hatred. The oversocialized person cannot even experience, without guilt, thoughts or feelings that are contrary to the accepted morality; he cannot think 'unclean' thoughts. And socialization is not just a matter of morality; we are socialized to conform to many norms of behavior that do not fall under the heading of morality. Thus the oversocialized person is kept on a psychological leash and spends his life running on rails that society has laid down for him. In many oversocialized people this results in a sense of constraint and powerlessness that can be a severe hardship. We suggest that oversocialization is among the more serious cruelties that human beings inflict on one another." – Excerpt from the Unabomber's Manifesto

Kaczynski at Harvard

Perhaps not surprisingly, Kaczynski did not fit in any better at Harvard than he had in high school. For most of his time there he lived in Eliot House, in a suite he shared with seven other young men, including Patrick McIntosh. McIntosh remembered, "I don't recall more than 10 words being spoken by him. ... Ted's room had a good view of the [Charles] river, but I never saw anybody live in such an unkempt place. In some places, the papers and such were a foot deep. That disturbed me, that someone could live in such filth. The worst part was when it began to smell. Maybe it was rancid milk. ... He was intensely introverted. He wouldn't allow us to know him. I never met anybody like him who was as extreme in avoiding socialization. He would almost run to his room to avoid a conversation if one of us tried to approach him."

Part of the problem may have been the difference between Kaczynski's social background and that of his other, wealthier and more athletic suite mates. According to classmate Richard Adams, "The whole varsity crew was in Eliot House. They were all very tall and athletic and preppie. Kaczynski and I weren't part of that. He was sallow, humorless, introverted, a guy who couldn't make conversation. Kaczynski wore non-modish clothes: a kind of unpleasant plaid sports jacket and a tie that didn't go with it. He didn't look happy. ... He was a wonk. He epitomized that. He felt fairly comfortable in that role."

After graduating from Harvard with a degree in Mathematics, Kaczynski enrolled in the University of Michigan at Ann Arbor in 1962, completing both Masters and Doctoral degrees there by the time he was 25. During his time there, he was pleased to be able to live alone and, it seems, to be left alone. One of his professors, Peter Duren, recalled, "Mathematics seemed to be the only thing he was interested in. ... A lot of mathematicians are a little bit strange in one way or another. It goes with creativity." Math was indeed the one area in which Kaczynski thrived, so much so that another professor, George Piranian, admitted, "He did not make mistakes. He was very persistent in his work. If a problem was hard, he worked harder. He was easily the top student, or one of the top."

Kaczynski's prowess was recognized by many more people than his professors. For their parts, his fellow students quickly realized that they did not stand a chance competing with him in any mathematical endeavor. Joel Shapiro, who became a mathematics professor, said, "While most of us were just trying to learn how to arrange logical statements into coherent arguments, Ted was quietly solving open problems and creating new mathematics. It was as if he could write poetry while the rest of us were trying to learn grammar."

In 1965, one of Kaczynski's papers, "Boundary Functions for Functions Defined in a Disk," was published by the *Journal of Mathematics and Mechanics*. The following year, he had another article, "On a Boundary Property of Continuous Functions," published in the *Michigan Mathematics Journal*. The works were as complex as they were cutting edge, leading one of his professors to observe, "I would guess that maybe 10 or 12 people in the country understood or appreciated it." His dissertation, "Boundary Functions," was so complex that even his professors admitted to not understanding portions of it, and it won him the prestigious Sumner B. Myers Prize for best dissertation in mathematics that year.

As much as he sought to remain isolated during the school year, Kaczynski hid himself away even more during the summers, often camping alone along Coralville Lake, near his parents' new home in Lisbon, Iowa. When he did return to town, he surprised the townsfolk with what he brought back. One young woman recounted one unusual episode: "He brought in a bunch of roots and weeds and things, and he was showing them to us. He said they were all good to eat. He told us that some of them tasted like potatoes. He was kind of shy and unusually quiet. But he didn't seem strange. I mean, the roots were edible."

Given his credentials, Kaczynski had no problem finding a job, and he eventually joined the Math Department at the University of California at Berkeley as an assistant professor, the youngest person ever hired in that position. However, he was notably conservative in the face of the "free love" era at Berkeley, leading him to bitterly claim, "Political correctness has its stronghold among university professors, who have secure employment with comfortable salaries, and the majority of whom are heterosexual white males from middle- to upper-middle-class families. ... Notice that university intellectuals constitute the most highly socialized segment of our society and also the most left-wing segment."

All the while, Kaczynski lived alone and rarely interacted with anyone except when teaching one of his classes, including "Numbers Systems," "Introduction to the Theory of Sets," and "General Topology and Function Spaces." With his eccentricities, it was almost inevitable that Kaczynski was not a very effective instructor. One of his students complained that he "absolutely refuses to answer questions." Nor did he get along with the faculty, according to Lance W. Small, who was also an assistant professor at Berkeley at the time: "I can go down and probably tell you something about every one of those people, and picture them in my mind. But I can't recollect this guy, nor does anybody I know recollect him." At the same time, Small also gave credit to Kaczynski for publishing several articles during his short time at Berkeley:"That's a very respectable output, and they're in very good journals."

Kaczynski at Berkeley in 1967

Kaczynski remained on staff at Berkeley until June 1969, when he suddenly stepped down, perhaps because of his inability to relate to his students. In spite of his limitations as an instructor, many working at the University were sorry to lose him and asserted that he could have had a successful career in research and writing. Professor John Addison was perplexed by Kaczynski's departure: "He said he was going to give up mathematics and wasn't sure what he was going to do. He was very calm and relaxed about it on the outside. We tried to persuade him to reconsider, but our presentation had no apparent effect. Kaczynski seemed almost pathologically shy, and as far as I know, he made no close friends in the department. ... I really think his views are a product of what was in the air in Berkeley in those days. You could become infected by this feeling that society had taken a wrong turn. Terrible things were going on, and you couldn't help but be affected."

When asked about his older brother's decision, David Kaczynski insisted, "It was not an antiwar gesture, something to do with the counterculture. Both of us were in love with nature. I assume he wanted to live a richer life. ... I think if he viewed [the turmoil] in any way at all, he viewed it as a fad. ... He was a person who seemed capable of closing doors on things, on people, on stages of his life. That cutting himself off was part of what he was about. At some point, it happened with me. At some point, it happened with our parents. As a kid, he loved his coin collection, and then he stopped collecting the coins. It was also true with a friend of his who would call in high school. 'Hi, it's Mosny. Is Ted around?' 'I don't want to talk to him.' You can expand that whole theme of cutting oneself off."

There Is No Stable Framework

"It is well known that crowding increases stress and aggression. The degree of crowding that exists today and the isolation of man from nature are consequences of technological progress. All pre-industrial societies were predominantly rural. The Industrial Revolution vastly increased the size of cities and the proportion of the population that lives in them, and modern agricultural technology has made it possible for the Earth to support a far denser population than it ever did before. (Also, technology exacerbates the effects of crowding because it puts increased disruptive powers in people's hands. For example, a variety of noise-making devices: power mowers, radios, motorcycles, etc. If the use of these devices is unrestricted, people who want peace and quiet are frustrated by the noise. If their use is restricted, people who use the devices are frustrated by the regulations. But if these machines had never been invented there would have been no conflict and no frustration generated by them.) For primitive societies the natural world (which usually changes only slowly) provided a stable framework and therefore a sense of security. In the modern world it is human society that dominates nature rather than the other way around, and modern society changes very rapidly owing to technological change. Thus there is no stable framework." – Excerpt from the Unabomber's Manifesto

After leaving Berkeley, Kaczynski persuaded his brother to drive with him to Canada in the hopes of finding some wilderness land to buy and live on. According to David, the two months they spent together proved pivotal to their relationship: "I had a year of college to finish up. I was purely accompanying him, to do something together as brothers. … I was very strongly influenced by my brother." In many ways, it would have been better for both men if David had been the one doing the influencing, because Ted was becoming increasingly depressed and withdrawn. David described the helplessness he felt trying to deal with his brother: "I saw this a number of times in his life. There must be something triggering it, but I didn't know what it was. Looking back, I'm not sure. I believe it was the day before he was to put in his application for this piece of land. He shut down for a day. There was no interaction. It was like he was unreachable."

At the end of the summer, David went back to school and Ted moved in with his parents, presumably in order to save money to build a home on the land he had applied for in Canada. Instead, he spent most of the year alone in his bedroom, rejecting all his parents' suggestions that he get a job or at least leave the house and do something. The only things he produced during this year consisted of a substantial number of letters to public figures and others complaining about the effects of modern American life on the environment. He developed a particular hatred of advertising, writing, "Advertising and marketing techniques have been developed that make many people feel they need things that their grandparents never desired or even dreamed of. It requires serious effort to earn enough money to satisfy these artificial needs.... Modern man must satisfy his need for the power process largely through pursuit of the artificial needs created by the advertising and marketing industry, and through surrogate activities. It seems that for many people, maybe the majority, these artificial forms of the power process are insufficient. A theme that appears repeatedly in the writings of the social critics of the second half of the 20th century is the sense of purposelessness that afflicts many people in modern society. (This purposelessness is often called by other names such as "anomic" or "middle-class vacuity.") We suggest that the so-called "identity crisis" is actually a search for a sense of purpose, often for commitment to a suitable surrogate activity. It may be that existentialism is in large part a response to the purposelessness of modern life. Very widespread in modern society is the search for "fulfillment." But we think that for the majority of people an activity whose main goal is fulfillment (that is, a surrogate activity) does not bring completely satisfactory fulfillment."

Among the letters that Kaczynski wrote during this period was one published in *The Saturday Review* on February 28, 1970, a rant about the growing number of cars and highways in America. Part of that letter read, "Perhaps a better solution would be to change the structure of society so that it becomes possible to allow people some of the freedom and independence that they seem to crave. A happily married man does not daydream about romantic love. Similarly, a man does not romanticize frontier freedom unless he is suffering from a lack of personal autonomy. Most of the problems are direct or indirect results of the activity of large organizations -- corporations and governments. It is these organizations, after all, that control the structure and development of society. Perhaps the most unfortunate thing that has ever happened to individual liberty was its being used as an excuse for the misdeeds of huge corporations."

When Ted learned that his land application had been rejected, David remembered that he "got very depressed. My sense is that it went on for a couple of months, and eventually he got a job. It was just a job to earn a little money, laborer or construction, something like that." Then, not long after David graduated and moved to Montana, Ted joined his brother and built a small cabin on a wooded, 1.4 acre plot he bought, despite the fact David had moved back to Iowa by that point. It's clear that the cabin offered Ted some of the freedom he claimed was being held out of reach of most people: "Industrial-technological society cannot be reformed in such a way as to prevent it from progressively narrowing the sphere of human freedom. ... By 'freedom' we mean the opportunity to go through the power process, with real goals not the artificial goals of surrogate activities, and without interference, manipulation or supervision from anyone, especially from any large organization. Freedom means being in control (either as an individual or as a member of a SMALL group) of the life-and-death issues of one's existence; food, clothing, shelter and defense against whatever threats there may be in one's environment. Freedom means having power; not the power to control other people but the power to control the circumstances of one's own life. One does not have freedom if anyone else (especially a large organization) has power over one, no matter how benevolently, tolerantly and permissively that power may be exercised.

It is important not to confuse freedom with mere permissiveness. ... The degree of personal freedom that exists in a society is determined more by the economic and technological structure of the society than by its laws or its form of government. Most of the Indian nations of New England were monarchies, and many of the cities of the Italian Renaissance were controlled by dictators. But in reading about these societies one gets the impression that they allowed far more personal freedom than our society does. In part this was because they lacked efficient mechanisms for enforcing the ruler's will: There were no modern, well-organized police forces, no rapid long-distance communications, no surveillance cameras, no dossiers of information about the lives of average citizens. Hence it was relatively easy to evade control."

For Kaczynski, freedom was found in that one-room, 120 square foot cabin he built on his land. His water came from the well he had dug with his own hands, his heat came from a wood stove, and his light came from the sun during the day and a kerosene lamp at night. Weather permitting, he cooked his meals outdoors in a fire pit. While those living in nearby Lincoln may have marveled at the thin, bearded man dressed in either black or army fatigues who occasionally came into town for supplies, they mostly left him alone. Rhoda Burke, who worked at the local grocery store, offered up an opinion of Ted shared by so many who encountered him: "He never would really offer any conversation. He'd come in once or twice a month and buy his staples and put them on the back of his bike and ride out of town." Kaczynski trips into town usually included a stop at the local library. According to librarian Beverly Coleman, "Sometimes he came in once a week because we saved newspapers for him and he picked them all up. Just our local tribunes, from Missoula and Great Falls and Helena." About the only people to ever visited Kaczynski's home during this time were the census takers who turned up once every decade. Joseph Youderian interviewed him briefly in 1990 and insisted, "He was just a private person and enjoyed being up there by himself. ... I didn't push it. That's the way he wanted to live."

Pictures of the cabin and its interior, now located in Washington, D.C.'s Newseum

Kaczynski largely lived off the land, making his own candles to read by and making his own bread to eat. He also gardened and hunted small game. Through it all, Kaczynski's frugality and careful record keeping allowed him to survive on just 30 cents a day, which came out to just over $100 a year. His parents supplied this and more in the form of very generous checks to him for his birthdays and during Christmas. When he needed money, he would find a short term job in construction or some other blue collar position.

In the spring of 1978, Kaczynski, shaven and clean, left his cabin and headed east to Chicago, where he is believed to have met with Donald Saari, a professor in the Mathematics Department at Northwestern University in Evanston. Though he never gave his name to Saari, the professor later claimed that it must have been Kaszynski: "The first time, he just arrived, standing shyly outside my door, and I invited him to come in. ... He was shy, his social graces were not the best and he tended to wear working clothes and working shoes. On the other hand, he did not have the firm handshake of someone from the working class."

Saari

This "working class" man was not there to learn but to teach; Kaczynski asked Saari to review a treatise he had written against technology. At the time, Saari thought to himself, "I'm dealing with a person that I think has a future, that should go back to school. He's expressing ideas amateurishly. They're not well defined or well thought out. But with going to school, they could be polished." Thus, Saari suggested that Kaczynski submit his paper to Chicago Circle at the University of Illinois, but when they rejected his manuscript, Kaczynski stormed back into Saari's office: "He was quite angry -- never raised his voice -- but he was enraged, and he was trembling. He told me that these highfalutin' Ph.D.'s had dismissed him from their offices. I guess they had looked over his manuscript and summarily dismissed him." Kaczynski's parting words, "I'll get even," proved prophetic, and the next time Saari saw him, it was at a lecture on the history of gunpowder.

The Consequences Will Still Be Very Painful

"If the system breaks down the consequences will still be very painful. But the bigger the system grows the more disastrous the results of its breakdown will be, so if it is to break down it had best break down sooner rather than later. We therefore advocate a revolution against the industrial system. This revolution may or may not make use of violence; it may be sudden or it may be a relatively gradual process spanning a few decades. We can't predict any of that. But we do outline in a very general way the measures that those who hate the industrial system should take in order to prepare the way for a revolution against that form of society. This is not to be a POLITICAL revolution. Its object will be to overthrow not governments but the economic and technological basis of the present society. … Some oversocialized leftists have gone so far as to rebel against one of modern society's most important principles by engaging in physical violence. By their own account, violence is for them a form of 'liberation.' In other words, by committing violence they break through the psychological restraints that have been trained into them. Because they are oversocialized these restraints have been more confining for them than for others; hence their need to break free of them. But they usually justify their rebellion in terms of mainstream values." – Excerpt from the Unabomber's Manifesto

Having his paper rejected hurt Kaczynski in a way that nothing else apparently ever had, and with that, he made the fateful decision to strike back. *The New York Times* later described the first bomb the Unabomber used: "The first device was quite crude, a piece of pipe that might have come from a kitchen sink. The explosive was gunpowder and shavings of wooden matchheads. The wire had been pulled from an old lamp cord, and the triggering device was simple and dangerous. But the container was almost a work of art, carefully fashioned from four kinds of wood, meticulously sanded, polished and stained, like a piece of fine furniture from an old-world artisan. The package was addressed to a professor at the Chicago Circle campus of the University of Illinois, where it was left in a parking lot on May 24, 1978. But instead of being forwarded to its addressee, it was returned to its apparent sender, a professor at Northwestern University. Since that person had not actually sent the package, it was turned over to Northwestern's campus security force. It exploded the next day, badly injuring a guard who opened it. It seems mere chance that the bomb went off at Northwestern in Evanston, rather than at the Chicago Circle campus of the University of Illinois. But the address and the return address on the package suggests that either may have been a satisfactory target to the Unabomber."

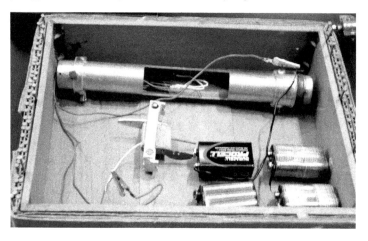

An FBI recreation of one of Kaczynski's bombs

As if that initial explosion had somehow exorcised some of his demons, Kaczynski returned home to Lombard and took a job at the plant where his father and brother already worked. He spent his days earning an honest living as a press operator and even expanded his social life by dating 29 year old Ellen Tarmichael, his supervisor. David said of this time, "He happened to see her car. She was filling the gas tank. I don't know exactly what transpired. He actually went to her apartment and played cards with her and her sister and her boyfriend. ... [When he came home] he was obviously in a really good mood. He told me he had gone to see Ellen, that they had spent the day together and had played cards, and that some gestures indicating affection had passed between them. I was very happy about that." On another occasion, the two went to a French restaurant, where Ted "ordered wine and he smelled it, he made a big deal of it. He had a good time."

Unfortunately, the relationship quickly ended as Tarmichael realized she was not interested in him, and David noted that, as he had before, "Ted did a total shutdown." To make matters worse, Kaczynski made copies of a nasty limerick he wrote about Tarmichael and posted them around the plant, which proved to be too much even for his younger brother: "I was very, very angry. Part of me was disappointed. He was so close to being integrated in the most primal rite of integration. He had an interest in a member of the opposite sex, and to have him go back to this kind of angry, inappropriate behavior -- to the family it was embarrassing, adolescent kind of behavior." David ordered Ted to take down the limericks, and when he refused, he fired his big brother.

As things between them grew increasingly uncomfortable, David left Lombard and moved to Texas, while Ted continued to live with his parents and, as it turned out, made his irreversible plunge into the life of a terrorist. His next attack was carried out on May 9, 1979, when he again left a bomb in a box at Northwestern University's Technological Institute. When student John Harris attempted to open the box, the bomb went off and injured him. Half a year later, on November 15, a bomb he mailed exploded aboard an American Airlines flight going from Chicago to Washington and came dangerously close to destroying it; the plane was forced to make an emergency landing as smoke entered the cabin.

Naturally, when these attacks started, no one dreamed that they had anything to do with a shaggy-haired mathematics genius. In fact, America was in the midst of the Iranian hostage crisis after revolutionaries took over the U.S. Embassy in Tehran, and Iran's new regime was immediately suspected. Further obscuring things, authorities received unsolicited tips from people taking credit for the attack, as the *Associated Press* reported: "The FBI said today it is investigating reports that a bomb which exploded aboard an American Airlines jetliner on a flight from Chicago to Washington, D.C., was the work of a pro-Iranian group. No one was injured in the incident. The group claiming responsibility for the incident in anonymous telephone calls to the news media here threatened more bombings if actions were taken against Iranians in the Chicago area. President Carter has ordered the investigation of the visa status of

Iranian students in the United States in response to the taking of some 60 American hostages at the U.S. Embassy in Tehran. Eighty passengers and crew members escaped the smoke-filled plane moments after American Flight 444 made an emergency landing Thursday afternoon at Washington's Dulles International Airport. The Chicago Tribune, and two television stations, WBBM and WMAQ reported receiving calls from a man claiming an Iranian students group was responsible for the bombing. The man, calling some 12 hours after the explosion, said he was a member of the group and threatened more bombings if actions were taken against Iranians in the Chicago area."

At some point during this period, Kaczynski returned to his self-appointed exile in the Montana woods, and it was from there that he planned his fourth attack. This one took place on June 10, 1980, when he mailed a bomb to the president of United Airlines, Percy Wood. According to an *Associated Press* article:

"Police say they have no leads on the origin of a package bomb that exploded in the home of United Airlines President Percy A. Wood, leaving him with 'extensive' cuts in his face, left hand and left leg. Wood, 60, was in good condition late Tuesday after surgery in Lake Forest Hospital. Police said a guard had been posted at the airline executive's hospital room. 'He said he didn't know why someone would do this to him,' said a neighbor who comforted the wounded executive. Chicago FBI spokesman George Mandich said the explosive was contained in 'not too big a package' delivered to Wood's home in the wealthy lakeshore suburb north of Chicago. No one claimed responsibility in the bombing, Mandich said. Police Chief Bernard Prais said whoever constructed the device 'had to know a little of what they were doing. It had to be triggered somehow and it had to be safe enough to get there.' Wood underwent surgery to remove bomb fragments from his face and hands. Doctors said Wood suffered 'no permanent damage,' according to hospital spokeswoman Joyce Fitzgerald. However, she said the cuts were extensive and Wood may require plastic surgery...

"FBI agents said the bomb, which exploded at about 3:48 p.m. EDT, apparently was delivered by mail. Prais said Wood told him the bomb was contained in a paper-wrapped package disguised as a book in his roadside mail box. The package exploded as Wood opened it in the kitchen, Prais said. Wood walked to the house of neighbors who summoned the ambulance and police. Laurie McCurdy, 17, said she and her mother, Anna Jean, were watching television when Wood appeared at the front door, his face bloodied. Miss McCurdy said she sat on the front porch with Wood and 'just sort of comforted him.' She said she saw that he had deep cuts on his face and hands and that his trousers were ripped open and soaked with blood. 'He told me he opened the package and it just blew,' she said. 'He said he didn't know why anyone would do something like this to him.' Prais said Wood told him he had no known enemies and had not received any threats or suspicious phone calls. Neighbors said Wood's wife, Mary, was in California on Tuesday, and that the couple's four sons all live away from home. United Airlines spokesman Marc Michaelson said Wood has been with the airline since 1941 and has been president and chief operating officer since December 1978. Neighbors said the Woods were well liked by residents of the winding, tree-lined street. Larry McCurdy, whose wife called the ambulance, said he could think of no motive for the bombing. 'There's a lot of things that occur to you when something like this happens,' said McCurdy, a manufacturing executive. 'The question that runs through your mind is why someone would want to do this to someone who, from our viewpoint, is just a nice human being.'"

When Kaczynski was arrested over 15 years later and accused of being the Unabomber, Percy Wood echoed the sentiments held by so many of his victims: "I've thought about it a lot but I still don't know why it happened. I've never heard the guy's name. I never saw him before."

Our Real Enemy

"Our real enemy is the industrial- technological system, and in the struggle against the system, ethnic distinctions are of no importance. The kind of revolution we have in mind will not necessarily involve an armed uprising against any government. It may or may not involve physical violence, but it will not be a POLITICAL revolution. Its focus will be on technology and economics, not politics. Probably the revolutionaries should even AVOID assuming political power, whether by legal or illegal means, until the industrial system is stressed to the danger point and has proved itself to be a failure in the eyes of most people. Suppose for example that some 'green' party should win control of the United States Congress in an election. In order to avoid betraying or watering down their own ideology they would have to take vigorous measures to turn economic growth into economic shrinkage. To the average man the results would appear disastrous: There would be massive unemployment, shortages of commodities, etc. Even if the grosser ill effects could be avoided through superhumanly skillful management, still people would have to begin giving up the luxuries to which they have become addicted. Dissatisfaction would grow, the 'green' party would be voted out of office and the revolutionaries would have suffered a severe setback. For this reason the revolutionaries should not try to acquire political power until the system has gotten itself into such a mess that any hardships will be seen as resulting from the failures of the industrial system itself and not from the policies of the revolutionaries. The revolution against technology will probably have to be a revolution by outsiders, a revolution from below and not from above." – Excerpt from the Unabomber's Manifesto

Throughout his reign of terror, Kaczynski remained in touch with his family, and though his letters to them took on an increasingly belligerent tone, when they visited him in person in his cabin, they found him to be polite and even affectionate. It was as if the bombs and his writings were the only outlets for his pent up anger. David observed, "With Ted, I have a sense of a person who appeared to deteriorate with time. I recall letters he wrote to our parents that were quite loving for quite a few years. How you get from that to some of the angry letters, I don't know. ... Ted always seemed interested to know about my experiences in the desert. He had told me on a number of occasions that Lincoln was getting too crowded. He felt stifled. I understand perfectly how he felt. A cabin coming up two miles away. It changes your lifestyle. Someone could look at you through binoculars, especially when your bathroom is outside. It could be a concern."

Meanwhile, Ted continued mailing bombs to various sites across the United States. Fortunately, his intended attack on the University of Utah failed when authorities were able to defuse the bomb before it went off on October 8, 1981, but Vanderbilt University in Tennessee was not so lucky on May 5, 1982. The *United Press International* reported, "A University of Pennsylvania return address is the vital clue to a mysterious letter bomb addressed to a Vanderbilt University computer science chairman that exploded and hospitalized a secretary, investigators say. The cigar-box-shaped wooden package exploded Wednesday and was addressed to Dr. Patrick Fischer, the head of the computer science department. The box was marked with a return address from the University of Pennsylvania, where Fischer taught until two years ago when he come to Vanderbilt. The secretary, Janet Smith, 39, was taken to nearby Vanderbilt Hospital with powder burns on her face and lacerations on her arms and chest. She was listed in stable condition after surgery to stitch up the cuts. Ms. Smith was sorting through the department's mail about 4 p.m. COT when she came across the package, said MacDonald Tweed of Vanderbilt's security staff. Tweed said the box exploded and landed three yards away from where it was opened, peppering the office with blood and bomb fragments. The bombing was Nashville's first since 1960."

Since the bombs were sent through the mail, the article pointed out that these were federal crimes: "U.S. Postal System inspectors are heading the investigation because the bomb was sent through the mail. Also involved in the investigation are the FBI, TBI, Nashville police, Vanderbilt security, and officials of the Alcohol, Tobacco and Firearms department. Tweed said the postal inspectors could trace the package and possibly come up with the person who mailed the bomb. Officials said the bomb was made of black powder and a detonating device. The bombing coincided with final spring semester examinations at Vanderbilt. Engineering department budget officer Hod Conner said the school usually gets threats on the days of important examinations. Fischer was in Europe and teaches high-level courses. He had no exams scheduled for Wednesday. Ms. Smith did not lose consciousness and a hospital spokesman said there were no complications and no loss of limbs or sight. 'In fact she's doing very well for someone who just got bombed,' the spokesman said. Conner found Ms. Smith seated in her office with blood on her chest and arms when he arrived. Powder burns covered her face and debris was scattered about the office. Conner said the room 'smelled like exploded firecrackers.' The bomb was relatively weak as letter bombs go, prompting speculation that the bomb did not completely detonate, Tweed said."

Perhaps feeding off what he considered his success, Kaczynski struck again on July 2, 1982, when he mailed one of his creations to Berkeley itself. The *Associated Press* reported, "A University of California electronics professor was injured today when a bomb exploded on the fourth floor of the campus engineering building, a university spokeswoman said Professor Diogenes J Angelakos. He was taken to Herrick Hospital where he was reported in fair condition with minor abrasions to his face and more serious injury to his hands There was no information on the source of the bomb, which reportedly caused minor damage when it went off at 7:49 a.m. in the coffee room of Cory Hall The building was briefly evacuated and searched for additional explosives, but none was found."

Angelakos

Following the Berkeley bombing, Kaczynski went quiet for a while, devoting himself to writing instead of violence, but the calm lasted for just a few years. In May of 1985, he mailed another bomb to the Berkeley, and this time it exploded in the hands of John Hauser, a graduate student who had the misfortune to be handling the mail that day. The *Associated Press* documented the grisly scene: "A graduate student suffered eye and arm injuries when a bomb exploded after he tried to open a package left in a building on the University of California campus. Police quickly evacuated and searched Cory Hall after the 1:45 p.m. explosion, which caused little structural damage. No other devices were found. The four-story building, which houses engineering and science classes, was to reopen today. John Hauser, 26, of Richmond, was listed in fair condition at Herrick Hospital, where he underwent surgery to repair damage to his right hand, arm and eye. Information officer Ron Treleven said "He was screaming, Help me! help me! "I went in and his arm was exploded. There was blood everywhere." said C C Chen, a graduate student working in an adjacent second-floor room. The device apparently was in a package left in a room used by computer students, said Prof D J J Angelakos, who was in a nearby room and talked, to the victim before he was taken to the hospital. "He opened it out of curiosity and it blew up, said Angelakos, a professor of engineering who suffered a similar injury three years ago when a package exploded on the fourth floor as he was examining it. On Tuesday, a pipe bomb was found in a classroom on the San Francisco State University campus. It was disarmed and partially detonated by authorities, and there were no injuries. Police Sgt. Robert Hulsey said an anonymous phone caller to the school security office at 7:30 a.m. warned that two bombs were planted on campus and said, "This is for flunking me." A janitor discovered the bomb at 5:50 a.m., but the call came before news of the event had been broadcast, Hulsey said. No second bomb was found."

The bomb at Berkeley put people on alert, so when Kaczynski sent a similar bomb to The Boeing Company in Auburn, Washington about a month later, it was discovered and defused without injuring anyone. However, when Psychology professor James V. McConnell of the University of Michigan opened a package addressed to him at his home on November 15, 1985 he and his research assistant were both injured. The wire services carried the story, writing, "A bomb mailed to a University of Michigan professor exploded when the instructor's research assistant opened the parcel, causing minor injuries, authorities said Sunday. Nicklaus Suino suffered arm and stomach injuries when he opened the package Friday at the home of psychology professor James McConnell, said Washtenaw County Sheriff's Dispatcher Sandra Watley. He was hospitalized overnight and released Saturday."

Up to this point, the bomber, known to police as "FC" for the initials he had carved on the bombs, was guilty of a number of crimes but was not yet a murderer. This changed on December 11, 1985, when a computer store owner in Sacramento opened a package. The *Associated Press* told readers, "Investigators have linked a fatal bombing last week to 10 other bombings or attempted bombings across the country since 1978, including one that exploded on an airplane in flight, officials said Thursday. One man killed in Sacramento was the only fatality but at least 19 people have been injured in the explosions, which have taken place in eight states and the District of Columbia. Sheriff Robbie Waters said at a news conference that the existence of the serial bomber had not been made public before. But Mike McCrystal, public information officer for the FBI here, said the FBI and the Postal Service had been working on the bombings since a device exploded on a plane flying from Chicago to Washington in November 1979. It detonated in the cargo compartment and caused 12 injuries by smoke inhalation, he said. The bombing here on Dec. 11 killed Hugh Scrutton, 38, owner of a computer rental store in a shopping center. The bomb was apparently left at the rear of the shop and Scrutton may have touched it when he went out the back door to go to the parking lot. Sheriff's Lt. Ray Biondi said the bombings were linked because of the similarity of the materials used."

Scrutton

Despite sending so many bombs in a short period of time, Kaczynski seemed to be the same as always by all outward appearances. In 1986, David visited Ted at his cabin in Montana, and while he found nothing in or around the cabin to indicate his brother had been up to anything illegal he had to concede in retrospect that his brother "wanted to be very specific about the day I was coming. ... He introduced me to people that he knew. I remember feeling pleased and reassured that he was a familiar character in town. ... [He] spent some time tutoring me in Spanish. He would have me read from some of the Spanish books. I had a sense that he really enjoyed doing that."

Certain Evils

"Even if medical progress could be maintained without the rest of the technological system, it would by itself bring certain evils. Suppose for example that a cure for diabetes is discovered. People with a genetic tendency to diabetes will then be able to survive and reproduce as well as anyone else. Natural selection against genes for diabetes will cease and such genes will spread throughout the population. (This may be occurring to some extent already, since diabetes, while not curable, can be controlled through the use of insulin.) The same thing will happen with many other diseases susceptibility to which is affected by genetic degradation of the population. The only solution will be some sort of eugenics program or extensive genetic engineering of human beings, so that man in the future will no longer be a creation of nature, or of chance, or of God (depending on your religious or philosophical opinions), but a manufactured product. If you think that big government interferes in your life too much NOW, just wait till the government starts regulating the genetic constitution of your children. Such regulation will inevitably follow the introduction of genetic engineering of human beings, because the consequences of unregulated genetic engineering would be disastrous." – Excerpt from the Unabomber's Manifesto

One thing that frustrated the FBI was how careful the man they now called the Unabomber was. He never left a fingerprint or licked a stamp, but there is no such thing as a perfect crime or a perfect criminal, and Kaczynski finally made a mistake on February 20, 1987, when a bomb he had left at a computer store in Salt Lake City, Utah went off. A woman noticed him and looked him in the eyes, causing him to panic and run away. This drew her attention, and she was able to give police a detailed description of the man who had dropped off the bomb. The authorities created a sketch that became instantly recognizable across the country and drove Kaczynski into hiding for the next six years.

The famous sketch of the Unabomber

Some of Kaczynski's clothing now on display

While Kaczynski kept a low profile and stopped sending bombs, he regularly corresponded with a man named Juan Sanchez Arreola, whom he never met in person but rather through mail, courtesy of David. Replying to Arreola's first letter, he wrote in careful Spanish, "I am pleased that you call yourself my friend. And I, in turn, call myself your friend." David remembered, "Ted said he didn't know what it was, but Juan touched him very deeply, and there are a number of instances throughout Ted's life when he was very, very deeply touched and sympathetic toward someone's pain he could understand, and Juan was one of these cases. ... He read about a millionaire who would receive requests for money and decide who to give it to. Ted decided this was the best way to get help for Juan, to pay his medical bills, and he drafted a letter that he sent to me. I was supposed to get an O.K. from Juan and send it to the millionaire. And of course, we never heard. For an intelligent person it seemed so…extremely naive."

Ted gained a friend in Arreola, but he lost further touch with his family, including David, who angered his older brother by marrying in 1991 and moving into mainstream society. Nonetheless, personal problems do not seem to be what drove him back to bombing as much as the February 1993 terrorist attack on the World Trade Center did. Almost as if that bombing send him into copycat mode, Kaczynski sent a bomb to Charles Epstein, a geneticist with the University of California. When Epstein opened the package on June 22, 1993, it exploded, blowing off three of his fingers and rendering him partially deaf. Two days later, David Gelernter lost his right hand

and much of the vision in his right eye when another Kaczynski creation exploded in his hands at Yale University. The *Associated Press* wrote, "A mail bomb severely injured a Yale University computer scientist Thursday, and the FBI was investigating a possible link to other explosions, including one that maimed a California professor this week. David Gelernter, 38, was opening his mail in his office at 8:15 a.m. when the explosion occurred, said John Sennett, an FBI spokesman. Later, after the bombing was reported on radio, someone called in a threat to the medical center where Gelernter's brother, a Yale geneticist, works. The bombing occurred just two days after a geneticist at the University of California-San Francisco, Dr. Charles Epstein, lost several fingers when a mailed package bomb exploded at his home. The FBI was looking for possible connections between the two cases and other recent bombings, 'both solved and unsolved,' Sennett said. ... FBI bomb examiner Christopher Ronay in Washington determined one bomber was behind the dozen incidents based on the meticulous handiwork employed. The FBI would not say Thursday whether the same person was suspected in this week's bombings. ... The FBI said authorities had to presume that David Gelernter was an intended target, although no motive was clear why he would be singled out. 'We're looking closely for any kind of motive, including those that are terrorist in nature,' Sennett said."

During this time, authorities and journalists thought the targets may be based on their political leanings. The article continued, "Gelernter, an associate professor and director of undergraduate studies in computer science, is an outspoken conservative, said a colleague, Professor Vladimir Rokhlin. Dr. Joel Gelernter, a Yale psychiatrist whose specialty is genetics, works at the Veterans Affairs Medical Center in neighboring West Haven. After the bombing, someone called the medical center switchboard and warned: '"You are next,'" said Louise FitzSimons, a VA spokeswoman. Federal agents checked Joel Gelernter's mail, but the hospital wasn't evacuated. Authorities said they did not immediately know the type of parcel or explosive used in the mail bomb. The blast caused David Gelernter severe wounds to the abdomen, chest, face and hands. He remained in critical condition Thursday evening at Yale-New Haven Hospital, said Tom Urtz, a hospital spokesman. Gelernter ran a block from his fifth-floor office to the university health clinic to get treatment, leaving, a trail of blood, authorities said. This week's other victim, Epstein, 59, was listed in fair condition at Marin General Hospital. The head of the medical genetics division at UC-San Francisco lost several fingers on his right hand and suffered burns, cuts and other injuries to the chest, abdomen and face when he opened a package bomb in his kitchen in Tiburon, north of San Francisco. The FBI said it was investigating because his research was funded by the National Institutes of Health. At Yale, the FBI was joined in the investigation by U.S. postal inspectors and agents from the Bureau of Alcohol, Tobacco and Firearms. Gelernter is well known in computer science for his work with parallel processing programming, and particularly for the programming language Linda, which he worked on as a graduate student at the State University of New York at Stony Brook."

Gelernter

Epstein

Following these attacks, Kaczynski went public for the first time, sending a letter to the *New York Times* in which he announced, "We are an anarchist group calling ourselves FC. Notice that the postmark on this envelope precedes a newsworthy event that will happen about the time you receive this letter, if nothing goes wrong. This will prove that we knew about the event in advance, so our claim of responsibility is truthful. Ask the FBI about FC. They have heard of us. We will give information about our goals at some future time. Right now we only want to establish our identity and provide an identifying number that will ensure the authenticity of any future communications from us. Keep this number secret so that no one else can pretend to speak in our name. 553-25-4394"

Kaczynski's next attack took place in December 1994, when he mailed a bomb to Thomas Mosser, an advertising executive living in North Caldwell, New Jersey. The bomb exploded on the 10th, and the *Associated Press* reported, "Thomas J. Mosser was a star in the advertising world, but went virtually unnoticed outside Madison Avenue. Now investigators and friends are trying to figure out what in the life of the 50-yearold Young & Rubicam Inc. executive could have caught the eye of a serial bomber. Mosser was killed in the kitchen of his home Saturday, apparently the latest victim of the 'Unabomber,' whose package bombs have killed one other man and injured 23 people since 1978. Mosser was [the] first victim who didn't work directly with universities, airlines or computers, and Young & Rubicam spokesman Richard McGowan said there's 'absolutely no suggestion' that the bombing was related to Mosser's work with the company or its clients. But Jim Freeman, FBI special agent in charge in San Francisco, said Monday that a link had not been ruled out. Investigators have been looking over Mosser's client list, and it appears he had some business with airlines, and computer giants Xerox Corp. and Digital Equipment Corp. recently hired Young & Rubicam. Investigators also are looking at whether the bomber might have seen trade articles about Mosser's Dec. 1 promotion to general manager, or a 1986 Fortune Magazine article naming Mosser as among 'people to watch' in business. The Unabomber has taunted investigators by stamping 'FC' on parts in most of the bombs, an apparent reference to a profane phrase denigrating computers. FBI experts have not yet found the initials on the bomb that killed Mosser. The FBI did say that the bomb had a return address from San Francisco State University and a Dec. 3 postmark from San Francisco."

Mosser

Kaczynski killed for the last time on April 24, 1995, when a bomb he sent exploded in the hands of Gilbert Brent Murray, a timber industry lobbyist. The *Associated Press* reported, "The Unabomber may have struck again, this time killing a timber industry executive who lobbied to have the spotted owl removed from the endangered species list. A heavy shoebox-sized package arrived by mail Monday at the California Forestry Association office. The package exploded when association president Gilbert Murray tried to open it, blowing out the windows and doors and scattering glass and ceiling tiles on the floor. Murray was killed in the reception area. Five others in the one story brick office building were not hurt. 'The similarities in the forensics preliminarily reviewed at the crime scene strongly suggest the Unabomber,' FBI Special Agent Richard Ross said Monday night after the federal Unabom task force took over the case. Before Monday, the Unabomber was believed to have carried out 15 bombings over 17 years. No one in U.S. history has set off as many bombs over as long a period of time. ... FBI investigators say the Unabomber, so called because his early targets were people connected to universities and airlines, appears to be fascinated with wood. Some of his bomb parts were carved out of wood, one victim was named Wood and twigs have been included in a bomb. The forestry association lobbies on behalf of wood products companies and timber owners. ... The package wrapped in brown paper was not addressed to Murray; authorities wouldn't say to whom it was sent. No warning was sent and no one claimed responsibility, said Sacramento police spokesman Michael Heenan. Police Chief Arturo Venegas said there was no indication the bombing was connected to last week's blast at the Oklahoma City federal building. ... 'We don't know what his motivation is. We don't know what his demands are. It's so damned difficult,' Rick Smith of the FBI's San Francisco office said recently."

Murray

Although nobody knew it yet, the attack on Murray would be the last attack the Unabomber got a chance to make.

Pressures

"Since the beginning of civilization, organized societies have had to put pressures on human beings of the sake of the functioning of the social organism. The kinds of pressures vary greatly from one society to another. Some of the pressures are physical (poor diet, excessive labor, environmental pollution), some are psychological (noise, crowding, forcing human behavior into the mold that society requires). In the past, human nature has been approximately constant, or at any rate has varied only within certain bounds. Consequently, societies have been able to push people only up to certain limits. When the limit of human endurance has been passed, things start going wrong: rebellion, or crime, or corruption, or evasion of work, or depression and other mental problems, or an elevated death rate, or a declining birth rate or something else, so that either the society breaks down, or its functioning becomes too inefficient and it is (quickly or gradually, through conquest, attrition or evolution) replaced by some more efficient form of society. Thus human nature has in the past put certain limits on the development of societies. People could be pushed only so far and no farther. But today this may be changing, because modern technology is developing ways of modifying human beings." – Excerpt from the Unabomber's Manifesto

After Murray's death, the *New York Times* soon heard from Kaczynski again, and this time he tried to explain himself: "We blew up Thomas Mosser last December because he was a Burston-Marsteller [sic] executive. Among other misdeeds, Burston-Marsteller [sic] helped Exxon clean up its public image after the Exxon Valdez incident. But we attacked Burston-Marsteller [sic] less for its specific misdeeds than on general principles. Burston-Marsteller [sic] is about the biggest organization in the public relations field. This means that its business is the development of techniques for manipulating people's attitudes. It was for this more than for its actions in specific cases that we sent a bomb to an executive of this company. Some news reports have made the misleading statement that we have been attacking universities or scholars. We have nothing against universities or scholars as such. All the university people whom we have attacked have been specialists in technical fields. (We consider certain areas of applied psychology, such as behavior modification, to be technical fields.) We would not want anyone to think that we have any desire to hurt professors who study archaeology, history, literature or harmless stuff like that. The people we are out to get are the scientists and engineers, especially in critical fields like computers and genetics. As for the bomb planted in the Business School at the U. of Utah, that was a botched operation. We won't say how or why it was botched because we don't want to give the FBI any clues. No one was hurt by that bomb."

The Unabomber also went on to clarify his political leanings: "We call ourselves anarchists because we would like, ideally, to break down all society into very small, completely autonomous units. ... Our more immediate goal, which we think may be attainable at some time during the next several decades, is the destruction of the worldwide industrial system."

Most notably, Kaczynski offered a deal to the paper: "We have a long article, between 29,000 and 37,000 words, that we want to have published. If you can get it published according to our requirements we will permanently desist from terrorist activities. It must be published in the *New York Times, Time* or *Newsweek*, or in some other widely read, nationally distributed periodical."

After discussing the decision with the FBI, the *Washington Post*, in cooperation with the *New York Times*, did indeed print Kaczynski's Manifesto in September 1995, part of which read, "So we don't claim that this article expresses more than a crude approximation to the truth. All the same we are reasonably confident that the general outlines of the picture we have painted here are roughly correct. We have portrayed leftism in its modern form as a phenomenon peculiar to our time and as a symptom of the disruption of the power process. But we might possibly be wrong about this. Oversocialized types who try to satisfy their drive for power by imposing their morality on everyone have certainly been around for a long time. But we THINK that the decisive role played by feelings of inferiority, low self-esteem, powerlessness, identification with victims by people who are not themselves victims, is a peculiarity of modern leftism. Identification with victims by people not themselves victims can be seen to some extent in 19th century leftism and early Christianity but as far as we can make out, symptoms of low self-esteem, etc., were not nearly so evident in these movements, or in any other movements, as they are in modern leftism. But we are not in a position to assert confidently that no such movements have existed prior to modern leftism. This is a significant question to which historians ought to give their attention."

As authorities hoped, the Manifesto proved to be Kaczynski's undoing. When David read the Manifesto, he noticed similarities between phrases in it and remarks his brother had made or written in the past. In February 1996, he reluctantly contacted the FBI and shared what he had discovered with the agency. Agents searched the shed outside the Kaczynski's previous home in Lombard and found trace materials that linked Ted to the early Unabomber attacks, after which they arrested Ted. The *New York Times* reported, "They might have been taken for hunters, if anyone had noticed them out in the snow. They had guns and binoculars, and they moved cautiously, like stalkers. They had rented rooms at a hotel in town in February, but people had been too nosy and they had moved to two cabins on a ridge up near the pass. Only Butch Gehring, who lived up there, knew who they were, and he had been sworn to secrecy. For 18 days, they watched, peering down through the winter woods with their binoculars and telescopes. Elk and deer, and once a cougar, crossed their lenses. But by late March, they had not seen the mountain man. They knew he often stayed in for weeks, but they began to wonder. Mr. Gehring was sent to check. He and a forest ranger confirmed that the hermit had not slipped away. ... They picked a cold, overcast day, April 3. Showers of snow and sleet fell from time to time. A mountain wind moaned and lifted the pine boughs. Canyon Creek gurgled with the spring melt. They formed a great circle, moving down the hillside and up the muddy road. Mr. Gehring went along. ... They used a little ruse. Mr. Gehring shouted, something about the ranger needing help to fix the line between their adjoining properties. The door opened, and a shaggy man stepped out. They took his arms from both sides. "Ted," one of them said. "We need to talk.""

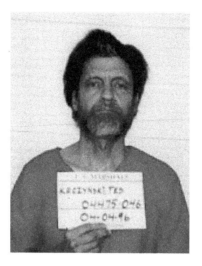

Kaczynski's mugshot

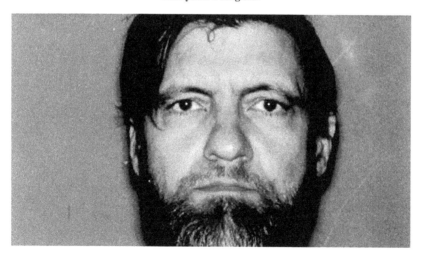

Kaczynski after his arrest

Naturally, Kaczynski's arrest made front page new across the country. The *Associated Press* reported, "Federal agents found a partially assembled bomb in the mountain snack of a former Berkeley math professor suspected of being the Unabomber, federal officials said. They prepared to charge him today. Ted John Kaczynski, 53, was to be charged with one count of possession of a bomb, according to three federal law enforcement officials.... The initial charge would hold Kaczynski but would make no mention of the Unabomber's 18-year string of bombing attacks while agents put together a detailed case. FBI and Bureau of Alcohol, Tobacco and Firearms agents found a partially assembled explosive device when they X-rayed one of many boxes in in his remote wilderness cabin late Wednesday.... They also said bomb diagrams were found. 'It's going very slowly because we're not sure if it's booby-trapped,' said one federal agent. 'We have an explosives ordnance team X-raying everything before we touch it.' Officials said the search of the cabin and an outbuilding could take several days. 'We've got all the time in the world now that he's in custody,' said one agent. Also found were chemicals that could be used in bombs, including aluminum, and two manual typewriters, the officials said. ... Kazcynski was taken into custody by federal agents Wednesday so they could search his cabin.... He was not immediately placed under arrest or charged."

   In spite of the fact Kaczynski always referred to a group in his writings, no other followers or conspirators were ever found. Charged with 10 counts of bomb making and mailing and 3 counts of murder, Kaczynski refused to allow his attorneys to enter an insanity plea, even though refusing it meant he could receive the death penalty. In the end, he entered a guilty plea and thus avoided execution, instead receiving 8 life sentences without the possibility of parole in the maximum security federal prison in Florence, Colorado. As the *Associated Press* put it, "The angry rantings of Theodore Kaczynski ended the deadly reign of the Unabomber. Word by venomous word, they also helped send him to prison for the rest of his life. Facing evidence that included diary pages filled with his own damning statements and told he could not defend himself in court, Kaczynski brought an end to the nation's longest serial bombing case Thursday with a few quiet words: 'Guilty, your honor.' Kaczynski pleaded guilty to 13 federal charges covering five bombings, including two deaths in Sacramento and one in New Jersey. The agreement resolves all federal charges against Kaczynski, who also admitted his role in Unabomber attacks for which he had not been charged. The 55-year-old mathematics professor turned mountain hermit entered the last-minute plea on the day a jury was finally to be sworn in and opening statements were to begin. The agreement came shortly after U.S. District Judge Garland Burrell Jr. ruled that Kaczynski could not fire his lawyers and represent himself. Had Kaczynski been convicted, the man diagnosed as a paranoid schizophrenic could have faced death by injection. The agreement calls for life in prison without parole when he is formally sentenced May 15. 'The Unabomber's career is over,' prosecutor Robert Cleary declared. ... Under the agreement, Kaczynski could also face $3.2 million in fines, and must forfeit any future earnings from the bombing campaign, including books, movies and memorabilia."

The supermax in Florence where Kaczynski is kept

Perhaps the best indication of how terrible and notorious Kaczynski's reign of terror was can be found by looking at the inmates he shares the supermax with, including jihadists like Zacarias Moussaoui who helped with 9/11, shoe bomber Richard Reid, 1993 World Trade Center bomber Ramzi Yousef, Oklahoma City bombing conspirator Terry Nichols, and underwear bomber Umar Abdulmutallab.

Not surprisingly, Kaczynski has remained a prolific writer in prison, keeping up correspondences with hundreds of people, and it seemed that his only regret about life in prison was that it could not match the woods: "No, what worries me is that I might in a sense adapt to this environment and come to be comfortable here and not resent it anymore. And I am afraid that as the years go by that I may forget, I may begin to lose my memories of the mountains and the woods and that's what really worries me, that I might lose those memories, and lose that sense of contact with wild nature in general. But I am not afraid they are going to break my spirit."

If Kaczynski is the least bit remorseful, he's kept it to himself. If anything, the last time he made headlines suggested he was proud of the crimes or at least not above taunting the public about it. In 2012, Kacyznski was included in a Harvard alumni directory, for which he had to provide information about his life. He wrote that his occupation was "Prisoner," and that his home address of "No. 04475-046, US Penitentiary—Max, P.O. Box 8500, Florence, CO 8126-8500." Under the awards section, the Unabomber wrote, "Eight life sentences, issued by the United States District Court for the Eastern District of California, 1998."

Timothy McVeigh

Chapter 1: Distaste for the Federal Government

"On April 19th, 1993, that's four years ago…there was another great tragedy in American history. It occurred at Waco, Texas. That's the day that many lives were lost when the Branch Davidian compound burned down. But it was more than just a tragedy to McVeigh. You'll hear testimony from McVeigh's friends that he visited Waco during the siege and that he went back after the fire and that he had already harbored a great dislike and distaste for the federal government. They imposed taxes and the Brady Bill, and there were various other reasons that he had disliked the federal government. But the tragedy at Waco really sparked his anger; and as time passed, he became more and more and more outraged at the government, which he held responsible for the deaths at Waco. And he told people that the federal government had intentionally murdered people at Waco, they murdered the Davidians at Waco. He described the incident as the government's declaration of war against the American people. He wrote letters declaring that the government had drawn, quote, 'first blood,' unquote, at Waco; and he predicted there would be a violent revolution against the American government. As he put it, blood would flow in the streets." – Joseph Hartzler, prosecutor in the case against McVeigh

In February 1993, President Bill Clinton had only been in office for a few weeks when one of the most important events of his presidency began to take shape. Ironically, it would involve a group that the vast majority of Americans had never heard of and knew absolutely nothing about.

The Branch Davidians were an obscure religious sect located in Texas, but members of the group led by David Koresh in Waco, Texas stockpiled enough weaponry to catch the attention of the federal government. The U.S. Bureau of Alcohol, Tobacco, Firearms and Explosives (ATF) ultimately decided to serve arrest and search warrants at the compound for the possession of illegal weapons, even though they fully expected it would require a raid that could potentially turn fatal.

The ATF hoped to use the element of surprise when it commenced the raid on February 28, but the Branch Davidians were ready for them, which led to an intense firefight between the two sides that resulted in the deaths of 4 ATF agents and a number of Branch Davidians. With that, the FBI got involved, and federal agents settled in for a standoff that would last about 50 days, trying everything from negotiating to using sleep deprivation tactics to coerce the Branch Davidians into ending the confrontation. Finally, on April 19, government agents breached the compound's walls and tried to use gas to flush the Branch Davidians out peacefully, but a series of fires broke out and quickly spread, killing the vast majority of the occupants inside, including many young children.

Naturally, controversy spread over how the siege ended; for example, while most believe the Branch Davidians intentionally started the fires as part of a mass suicide, others insist it was the fault of the ATF. Debate also raged over whether the government could have and should have made different decisions to defuse the situation. As Alan Stone put it in a study of the siege,

"The tactical arm of federal law enforcement may conventionally think of the other side as a band of criminals or as a military force or, generically, as the aggressor. But the Branch Davidians were an unconventional group in an exalted, disturbed, and desperate state of mind. They were devoted to David Koresh as the Lamb of God. They were willing to die defending themselves in an apocalyptic ending and, in the alternative, to kill themselves and their children. However, these were neither psychiatrically depressed, suicidal people nor cold-blooded killers. They were ready to risk death as a test of their faith. The psychology of such behavior—together with its religious significance for the Branch Davidians—was mistakenly evaluated, if not simply ignored, by those responsible for the FBI strategy of 'tightening the noose'. The overwhelming show of force was not working in the way the tacticians supposed. It did not provoke the Branch Davidians to surrender, but it may have provoked David Koresh to order the mass-suicide." In 1999, a report prepared by the federal government itself concluded, "The violent tendencies of dangerous cults can be classified into two general categories—defensive violence and offensive violence. Defensive violence is utilized by cults to defend a compound or enclave that was created specifically to eliminate most contact with the dominant culture. The 1993 clash in Waco, Texas at the Branch Davidian complex is an illustration of such defensive violence. History has shown that groups that seek to withdraw from the dominant culture seldom act on their beliefs that the endtime has come unless provoked."

No matter which side people came down on, the violent confrontation embarrassed government officials, and Dick Morris, an advisor of Clinton's, even claimed that Attorney General Janet Reno only kept her job after Waco by threatening to pin the blame on the president: "[H]e went into a meeting with her, and he told me that she begged and pleaded, saying that . . . she didn't want to be fired because if she were fired it would look like he was firing her over Waco. And I knew that what that meant was that she would tell the truth about what happened in Waco. Now, to be fair, that's my supposition. I don't know what went on in Waco, but that was the cause. But I do know that she told him that if you fire me, I'm going to talk about Waco."

A picture of the Waco siege

While the world watched in horror as the Branch Davidian Compound went up in smoke on April 19, 1993, no one was aware that there was a man standing in the shadows who would bring about another conflagration just two short years later. Timothy McVeigh, the product of an unloving, broken home, was a self-professed "survivalist" and a student of such books as *The Turner Diaries*, a novel raving against the United States and urging others to overthrow its government.

McVeigh

   Although McVeigh held these sentiments from an early age, he still joined America's armed forces. In fact, he met Terry Nichols and Michael Fortier while in basic training in Georgia, and they had remained close throughout their time in the military, including serving together again at Fort Riley, Kansas. Prosecutor Joseph Hartzler summed up the relationships between the men: "Timothy McVeigh grew up in upstate New York; and after high school, he joined the Army. He first went to Fort Benning in Georgia, and that's where he met Terry Nichols. They served in Fort Benning in the same platoon. After he and Nichols completed their basic training at Fort Benning, they were both sent to Fort Riley, in Kansas. They became friends, in part because they both shared a distaste for the federal government. McVeigh's dislike for the federal government was revealed while he was still in the Army. Even at that early time in his life, he expressed an enthusiasm for this book *The Turner Diaries*. ... It follows the exploits of a group of well-armed men and women who call themselves 'patriots,' and they seek to overthrow the federal government by use of force and violence. In the book they make a fertilizer bomb in the back of a truck and they detonate it in front of a federal building in downtown Washington, D.C., during business hours and they kill hundreds of people. Friends, acquaintances, and family members of McVeigh will testify that he carried the book with him, gave copies to them, urged them to read this book."

   While Nichols had left the Army in 1989, McVeigh stayed in and spent four months in the Persian Gulf. He also took a month of training for Special Forces, thinking he might make the Army his career, but his zeal waned and he left the service in December 1991. At that point, McVeigh moved in with his father in Buffalo and got a job with a security company that was proud to hire a man who had served his country.

Nichols

Fortier

Hiring a former veteran may have pleased the company, but McVeigh was becoming less proud of his service, and of his country. He became increasingly depressed and obsessed with

American politics, especially over what he saw as government incursions on his freedom. Over time, he began writing increasingly angry letters to politicians in his district, protesting everything from meatpacking practices to laws concerning carrying mace. For instance, in February 1992 he wrote to Congressman John LaFalce, "Recently, I saw an article in the Buffalo News that detailed a man's arrest; one of the charges being 'possession of a noxious substance' (CS gas). This struck my curiosity (sic), so I went to the New York State Penal Law. Sure enough, section 270 prohibits possession of any noxious substance, and included in section 265 is a ban on the use of 'stun guns'. Now I am a male, and fully capable of defending myself, but how about a female? I strongly believe in a God-given right to self-defense. Should any other person or a governing body be able to tell a person that he/she cannot save their own life, because it would be a violation of the law? In this case, which is more important: faced with a rapist/murderer, would you pick a.) die, a law abiding citizen or b.) live, and go to jail? It is a lie if we tell ourselves that the police can protect us everywhere, at all times. I am in shock that a law exists which denies a woman's right to self-defense. Firearms restrictions are bad enough, but now a woman can't even carry mace in her purse?!?!"

McVeigh also pressed his friends to share his ideas, including encouraging them to read *The Turner Diaries*. In the summer of 1992, he traveled to Michigan and stayed with Terry Nichols, who had also become disenchanted with the American government and had even gone so far as to renounce his citizenship, writing, "I am no longer a citizen of the corrupt political corporate state of Michigan and the United States of America." Together, the men followed the story of the FBI's raid on the home of survivalist and white separatist Randy Weaver in Ruby Ridge, Idaho in August 1992. Several people were killed during the raid, including Weaver's wife and teenage son. Weaver finally surrendered, but the government's reputation was severely tarnished and men like McVeigh were incensed.

Now thoroughly in the throes of the survivalist movement, McVeigh moved to Lockport, New York. He got a job with another security company but did not stay with it long, leaving in January 1993 to sell guns around the country. One gun collector later recalled to investigators how obsessed McVeigh was with *The Turner Diaries*: "He carried that book all the time. He sold it at the shows. He'd have a few copies in the cargo pocket of his cammies. They were supposed to be $10, but he'd sell them for $5. It was like he was looking for converts…He could make 10 friends at a show, just by his manner and demeanor. He's polite, he doesn't interrupt."

In the process, McVeigh met a fellow gun enthusiast named Roger Moore. The two discussed the ATF's February 28 raid in Waco and agreed that the government was becoming much too powerful. Angry, McVeigh decided to go to Texas and see things for himself.

Michelle Rausch was a journalism student at Southern Methodist University when she heard about the standoff in Waco, and she decided to head out to the compound to see for herself what was happening. By doing so, she became the one human connection between two historic events.

She later testified, "I was writing for the school paper and had kind of been following the Waco standoff, and I knew there was another angle to the story, and I wanted to find what that angle was. ... So I took it upon myself during my spring break to travel to Waco to find what other angle to the, quote, 'Davidian standoff' there might be. ... This is how I found Mr. McVeigh, when I walked up on the hill. He was sitting on the hood of his car with some bumper stickers that were for sale. ... One of them I recall -- I can't see them clearly in this picture -- but Fear the Government that Fears Your Gun, Politicians Love Gun Control. ... I told him who I was and I was doing a story for my school paper and asked him why he was there. ... He said he just come in response to the standoff and that he -- he went on to say that he was opposed to how they handled the initial raid, that he thought it would be more appropriate had just the local sheriff gone down and issued an arrest warrant. ... He had a lot of views that he shared with me, which is -- as a writer and a journalist, I enjoyed speaking with him to write about his views in my article."

Later, Rausch was asked to share with the court some of the quotes from McVeigh that she used in her article. "The first quote: I think if the sheriff served the warrant, it would all be okay. They're not tactical at all. They're government employees. This was in reference to the ATF. Next one: It seems like the ATF just wants a chance to play with their toys, paid for by government money. The next direct quote: The government is afraid of the guns people have because they have to have control of the people at all times. Once you take away the guns, you can do anything to the people. You give them an inch and they take a mile. I believe we are slowly turning into a socialist government. He said, The government is continually growing bigger and more powerful, and the people need to prepare to defend themselves against government control."

Rausch concluded her remarks by telling the court, "McVeigh said a sheriff should have served the warrant to Koresh without involving the ATF. Although McVeigh said he is sorry for those killed and injured, he said the ATF had no business being there in the first place. McVeigh said those in the ATF were merely pawns working under the control of government orders. The government thinks it has to spend taxpayer dollars on something, McVeigh said, adding that they saw this as an opportunity and seized it. McVeigh said he believes the government is greatly at fault in Waco and has broken constitutional laws. He quoted the U.S. Constitution and said U.S. armed forces should not be used against civilians, yet they were used against Koresh and his followers. McVeigh said he does not believe the Brady Bill is a solution or an adequate attempt at a compromise. McVeigh said the Koresh standoff is only the beginning and that people should watch the government's role and heed any warning signs."

McVeigh did not remain in Texas long during the siege. Instead, he traveled again to Michigan to visit Nichols, and the two men watched the final days of the Waco stand-off unfold on television, including the tragic April 19 raid on the building where the Branch Davidians were holed-up. When fires broke out inside, the two men joined many others in the country in believing the government was ultimately responsible.

Chapter 2: Fertilizer Fuel-Based Bomb

"As his hatred of the government grew, so did his interest in a knowledge of explosives. You'll hear that he and Terry Nichols had experimented with small explosives on Nichols' farm in Michigan. Later our evidence will prove that McVeigh graduated to larger bombs, and you'll hear about an incident that occurred just one year before the bombing in a desert in Arizona where he made and detonated a pipe bomb. He placed it near a large boulder in the desert, and he ran away as the pipe bomb exploded and cracked the boulder. You will see that he also educated himself about how to build bombs, particularly truck bombs, using ammonium nitrate fertilizer and some sort of fuel oil. And we'll explain to you how you can make a bomb from fertilizer and fuel oil, and of course that's consistent with the type of destructive device that was used in Oklahoma City...he also obtained what was really a cookbook on how to make bombs. He ordered the book through the mail, we will show you; and the book is called Home Made C4. C4 is a type explosive. Some of you with military background know that. This book provides essentially a step-by-step recipe as to how to put together your own fertilizer fuel-based bomb." – Joseph Hartzler, prosecutor in the case against McVeigh

"A man with nothing left to lose is a very dangerous man and his energy/anger can be focused toward a common/righteous goal. What I'm asking you to do, then, is sit back and be honest with yourself. Do you have kids/wife? Would you back out at the last minute to care for the family? Are you interested in keeping your firearms for their current/future monetary value, or would you drag that '06 through rock, swamp and cactus...to get off the needed shot? In short, I'm not looking for talkers, I'm looking for fighters...And if you are a fed, think twice. Think twice about the Constitution you are supposedly enforcing (isn't "enforcing freedom" an oxymoron?) and think twice about catching us with our guard down – you will lose just like Degan did – and your family will lose." – A letter written by McVeigh to Steve Colbern, one of his customers

Not surprisingly, Waco only fueled the two men's hatred of the government, and shortly thereafter, while traveling with his gun business to Kingman, Arizona, McVeigh met up again with Fortier. McVeigh began to talk to Fortier about his belief that it was time to overthrow the government by any means necessary, and he introduced Fortier to *The Turner Diaries*. Fortier in turn introduced McVeigh to marijuana and crystal meth.

Together, the two discussed forming a militia group, and McVeigh remained in Kingman for the rest of the summer, working as a security guard. According to Fortier, "Somewhere along the line at one of the gun shows, he found a tape called, 'Waco, The Big Lie,' which we viewed at my house. We discussed the tape. Mostly we just rehashed the same old discussion over and over again. [He said those people were] Murdered and that there was a cover-up, that somebody should be held accountable."

In March 1994, McVeigh met with Andreas Strassmeir, head of a private militia based at Elohim City, a private community in Oklahoma founded by right-wing extremists. The two men stayed in touch, even while McVeigh continued to live in Kingman. By this time, McVeigh had become increasingly militant in his attitude toward the government; he created a bunker around his home in Arizona, began making and testing bombs, and on March 16, 1994, he renounced his citizenship.

A few months later, in July, McVeigh and Fortier started stealing regularly from the local National Guard Armory. Fortier later admitted, "One day at work Tim approached me and said that he had been noticing on his way to work each morning that there was a buildup happening at the local National Guard armory. He said over a period of days there is just more and more vehicles being parked in the back area. He asked me if I wanted to go with him one night to go check it out, which I did in the middle of the night. Me and Tim went and jumped the back fence, looked in the back of all the vehicles, and we looked at the bumper numbers. We just scouted around to see if there was any evidence of UN activity. ... We were peeking in the back of the trucks. They were all empty. As we were leaving, I came across some . . . a couple shovels, a couple picks, and two axes, which we stole. They were located on the undercarriage of a Humvee, which is like a Jeep. We had to hide underneath the Jeep because there was a diesel getting off the highway, and its lights flashed across the National Guard armory's yard, and we did not want to be seen, so we slid underneath the Jeeps; and that's when I noticed that they were there. And we just, on the spur of the moment, decided to take them."

Even stranger, McVeigh and Fortier began sneaking into the famous government site known as Area 51 in Roswell, New Mexico. However, they were not looking for aliens but for signs the government was getting ready to impose martial law.

In September 1994, McVeigh left Oklahoma and visited Gulfport, Mississippi. McVeigh seemed to have heard a rumor that there were United Nations troops massing along the Mississippi coast, so he went to see for himself if there was evidence for this. Though he found none, that did nothing to allay his fears of a One World Government. In fact, later that month, McVeigh went to Elohim City to participate in military exercises with the militia there.

It was during his weekend at Elohim City that McVeigh began to openly discuss a plan to detonate a large bomb at the Murrah Federal Building in Oklahoma City. According to Prosecutor Joseph Hartzler, "Over time McVeigh's anger and hatred of the government kept growing; and in the late summer of 1994...he decided that he had had enough. He told friends that he was done distributing antigovernment propaganda and talking about the coming revolution. He said it was time to take action, and the action he wanted to take was something dramatic, something that would shake up America, he said, and would cause ordinary citizens, he thought, to engage in a violent revolution against their democratically elected government.... The action he selected was the bombing, and the building he selected was the federal building in

Oklahoma City. ... And he offered two reasons for bombing -- or for selecting that particular building; first he thought that the ATF agents, whom he blamed for the Waco tragedy, had their offices in that building. ...second, he described that building as, quote, 'an easy target.' It was conveniently located just south of Kansas and it had easy access. It was just a matter of blocks off of an interstate highway, Interstate 35 through Oklahoma City traveling north; and the building is designed is such that you can drive a truck up, there is an indentation at the sidewalk in front of the building. You can drive a truck right up and park a truck right there in front of the building, right there in front of the plate glass windows...of the day-care center."

After leaving Elohim City, McVeigh traveled to Herington, Kansas, where he rented a storage unit, and on September 30, he bought a ton of ammonium nitrate, a fertilizer that he would later use to make the bomb for the Murrah Building. A few days later, on October 3, McVeigh stole dynamite and blasting caps from a nearby quarry.

In October, McVeigh returned to Michigan to see Nichols for a bit before they both headed back to Elohim City. From that time forward, McVeigh began using the alias Tim Tuttle to buy up large quantities of nitromethane, a powerful chemical used as a fuel in drag racing, among other things. It is also an important ingredient for making explosives and at the time was available in larger hobby shops because it was also used by radio controlled vehicle hobbyists.

During mid-October, McVeigh and Nichols spent two weeks in Arizona before returning to McPherson and purchasing another ton of fertilizer. Fortier later testified, "We got into a storage locker that they had rented, and Tim showed me some explosives that were inside it. I don't recall exactly the explosives I seen that night. What I recall, Tim had a flashlight, and the main part of the beam was shining on the box; and it had a -- and one of those orange triangles or yellow triangles -- not a triangle. Excuse me -- a diamond that says 'explosives.' That's what I remember seeing mostly. Tim was reaching into the box and showing me some explosives, but I don't remember exactly what it was he showed me. ...he was squatted down before a blanket that was covering some items that appeared to be more of the boxes containing explosives. I could estimate there were about three high, two and two deep. That would be about 12 boxes."

On October 20, McVeigh and Nichols made their first trip to the building they would soon target for destruction. They stopped their car in front of the Murrah Federal Building and then used a watch to time how far away McVeigh could get before the bomb went off. The next day, McVeigh went to Dallas and, disguised as a biker, bought $3,000 worth of nitromethane. He and Nichols then joined Fortier in Kingman, where the two men devoted themselves to perfecting their explosive mixture for maximum damage. Fortier's wife, Lori, later testified about one of these experiments: "One day me and Michael went over to Tim's house in Golden Valley, and he was in the process of finishing making a pipe bomb; and he asked us to go up in the mountains and blow it off with him. ...it was approximately a foot, foot and a half long, a couple inches in diameter, and it was made up of gun powder. And when we got there, he was putting the cap on it, on the end of it. ... We drove to an area between Golden Valley and Laughlin, Nevada. It's a mountain range called Union Pass, and we walked up about a mile, maybe 2 miles into the mountains. ... We walked into the mountains, and Tim put it under a boulder and set it off. ... [There was] A big cloud of smoke, and Tim and Mike went up there to look at what happened to the boulder, and it split in half."

Building this bomb was expensive work, and McVeigh and Nichols soon realized that they would have to come up with some way to finance their plot. Therefore, in November 1994, they found some men willing to break into a house and steal a number of valuable items that they then sold. The following month, McVeigh himself committed a number of robberies.

About this time, McVeigh took Fortier to the Federal Building in Oklahoma City to show him the target he had chosen. Fortier explained, "Well, we left Amarillo, and we were driving up to Kansas; and as we passed through Oklahoma City, Tim got off the highway saying he wanted to show me the building. ... We drove by the back of the building first...I'm speaking of the federal building Tim was pointing out. ...Tim asked me if I thought that a truck of the size he was speaking of would fit in the -- I'm not sure what it -- it looks like a commercial -- like a drop-off zone or just a little pull-in that's in front of the building. And I said, 'Yeah, you could probably fit three trucks in the front there.' And he drove further on, and then we turned into an alley, and he pointed out a spot where he was going to park his vehicle there. ... He said he was thinking of doing one of two things: One being Terry would follow him down in the morning, that he was planning this, and wait for him in this parking spot, or that they would drop a vehicle off there a couple days earlier and then Tim would just drive the truck down, himself, and then run to the car and get in it and drive away. ...I asked Tim why he wouldn't park closer.... And he said he didn't want to do that because he wanted to have a building between him and the blast."

Once they were back in Kansas, McVeigh and Nichols continued to perfect their plans for the attack, and in February 1995, they moved their bomb making material twice, first to a storage unit McVeigh rented in Herington, Kansas, and then to Fortier's home in Arizona. By this time, Strassmeir and a man named Dennis Mahon had also become interested in possibly bombing some large government facility in Oklahoma City. However, they were not as discreet as McVeigh was, so they eventually came to the attention of ATF agent Carole Howe. After a number of discussions between the ATF, the FBI, and the Attorney's General's office, the ATF decided not to raid Elohim City but to wait for more information. It is possible if not likely that the agency's decision was influenced by the previous disaster in Waco.

In March, just a month before the attack, Nichols began having second thoughts. He decided that while he was comfortable with helping McVeigh develop the bomb, he did not want to be around when McVeigh used it. McVeigh was disappointed but still went forward with his plan. According to Lori Fortier, "I was at the house, and he came and asked if he could use the typewriter; and I let him take it for a couple days. He brought it back a few days after that; and when he brought it back, he asked if he could use the iron, because he had something to laminate. And I told him no because I didn't want him to ruin our iron. So I took what it was that he had and I laminated it for him. It was a false driver's license. It was white. It had like a blue strip across the top, and Tim had put his picture on there. And it was like the false name of Robert Kling. I believe it was a North Dakota license. ... We made a joke about, like Star Trek and Klingon. It was something that was from Star Trek, so we made a joke about the name."

On April 5, McVeigh called someone in Elohim City. This person later became known as John Doe #2, but they have never been identified. Meanwhile, around this time, Fortier also decided to back out of the plan. As Lori later recounted in her testimony, "It was the first week of April, and me and Michael went to the Imperial Motel. Michael had a book that Tim had loaned him. Tim said that he wanted Michael to read the book, and Mike was giving the book back to him. We were scared of Tim, so Mike brought his gun with him at that time...we weren't really friends anymore, and we were really scared of him. ...he had told us everything about this, and we wanted out; and we thought he'd kill us because he had told us about it. [We were there] just a few minutes. We walked in, gave him the book, and we left."

Undeterred, McVeigh remained in Kingman for the next week, and at one point he visited a strip club in nearby Tulsa with Strassmeir and Michael Brescia. The government later investigated videotape from that night, and the investigation discovered that McVeigh had ominously told one dancer, "On April 19, you'll remember me for the rest of my life."

Chapter 3: A Catastrophic Explosion

"ATF, all you tyrannical people will swing in the wind one day for your treasonous actions against the Constitution of the United States. Remember the Nuremberg War Trials." – Excerpt from a letter written by McVeigh to the ATF shortly before the attack

"At 9:02 that morning...a catastrophic explosion ripped the air in downtown Oklahoma City. It instantaneously demolished the entire front of the Murrah Building...dismembered people inside, and it destroyed, forever, scores and scores and scores of lives, lives of innocent Americans...All the children I mentioned earlier, all of them died, and more; dozens and dozens of other men, women, children, cousins, loved ones, grandparents, grandchildren, ordinary Americans going about their business. And the only reason they died, the only reason that they are no longer with us, no longer with their loved ones, is that they were in a building owned by a government that Timothy McVeigh so hated that with premeditated intent and a well-designed plan that he had developed over months and months before the bombing, he chose to take their innocent lives to serve his twisted purpose. In plain, simple language, it was an act of terror, violence, intend -- intended to serve selfish political purpose. The man who committed this act is sitting in this courtroom behind me, and he's the one that committed those murders. After he did so, he fled the scene; and he avoided even damaging his eardrums, because he had earplugs with him." – Joseph Hartzler, prosecutor in the case against McVeigh

On April 13, McVeigh made yet another visit to Oklahoma City, this time to find a place where he could leave his car after the attack. He also visited his storage shed in Herington and verified that he had all the supplies he needed. The next day, he bought a 1977 Mercury Marquis and called to reserve a Ryder truck. He met Terry Nichols at nearby Geary Lake to get some more money and then checked into the Dreamland Motel in Junction City.

On April 16, he met Nichols in Herington and the two men drove to Oklahoma City. McVeigh left his Marquis near the Murrah building and Nichols drove him back to Kansas.

The following day, McVeigh picked up his reserved Ryder truck and drove it back to the Dreamland Motel, where he was still staying. Early on the morning of the 18th, he drove the truck to his storage unit, where Nichols came to meet him, and together the two men loaded the bags of fertilizer and the drums of nitromethane into the back of the truck. Lori Fortier subsequently testified about a conversation they had once had about the way McVeigh would set up the bomb in the truck: "He wasn't sure whether he was going to drill holes into the cab of the truck, or if the truck had windows, he was going to like just put them through the windows. The fuse. There would be two separate fuses. ... He used the term 'shape charge.' ... By drawing the barrels in the truck, he formed them in a triangle shape with the biggest part of the triangle would be facing the building to get the most...impact.... He said that he and Terry would do it together; that Terry would mix the bomb. ... He had a book that had the different detonation ratios, I guess you'd call it, of different types of explosives."

Next, the two men drove to Geary Lake, where they could mix the explosive chemicals without being watched. From there, McVeigh drove alone to Ponca City, Oklahoma, where he parked his truck and slept for the night.

McVeigh awoke early on the morning of April 19 and left Ponca City around 7:00 a.m., headed for Oklahoma City and his massive attack. That same morning, as prosecutor Joseph Hartzler pointed out, parents were dropping off children at the daycare center inside the Murrah Federal Building: "When [Helena Garrett] turned to leave to go to her work, Tevin, as so often, often happens with small children, cried and clung to her; and then, as you see with children so frequently, they try to help each other. Little -- one of the little Coverdale boys -- there were two of them, Elijah and Aaron. The youngest one was two and a half. Elijah came up to Tevin and patted him on the back and comforted him as his mother left. As Helena Garrett left the Murrah Federal Building to go to work across the street, she could look back up at the building; and there was a wall of plate glass windows on the second floor. You can look through those windows and see into the day-care center; and the children would run up to those windows and press their hands and faces to those windows to say goodbye to their parents. And standing on the sidewalk, it was almost as though you can reach up and touch the children there on the second floor. But none of the parents of any of the children that I just mentioned ever touched those children again while they were still alive."

McVeigh got into town around 8:50 and drove straight for the Murrah Federal Building. He drove up NW 5th Street and lit the two fuses for his bomb. He then parked his truck in front of the building, locked it, and walked away from the site to his getaway car. Two minutes later, at exactly 9:02 a.m., the truck exploded.

An aerial view of the building

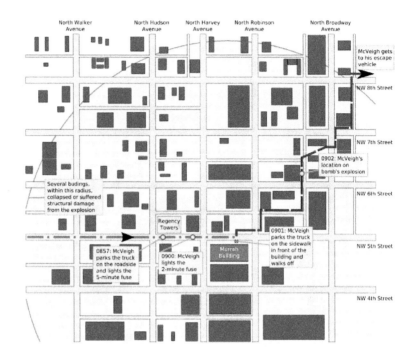

A map of the area and the route McVeigh took to get away

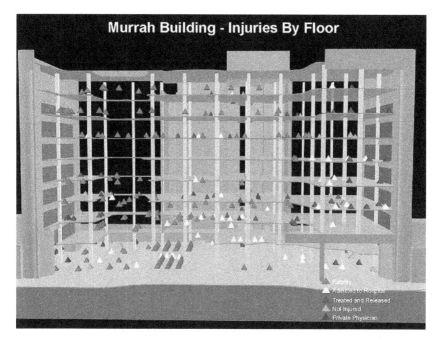

A graphic indicating the location of the dead and injured

The day care center in the Murrah Federal Building was nearest to where McVeigh parked the truck, so most of the children there were killed instantly. When he was later asked if he and McVeigh ever discussed the inevitable deaths that would result, Fortier answered, "I asked him about that... I said, 'What about all the people?' And he explained to me, using the terms from the movie 'Star Wars' -- he explained to me that he considered all those people to be as if they were the storm troopers in the movie 'Star Wars.' They may be individually innocent; but because they are part of the -- the evil empire, they were -- they were guilty by association." Apparently, McVeigh failed to explain how the children were guilty or why he chose to park the Ryder truck right in front of the daycare center.

Regardless, within a split second of the massive explosion, the rest of the building also began to collapse. One reporter who interviewed people at the building that day described the scene: "First the ceiling collapsed. Then the wires fell. Next the pipes sagged, broke and crashed down, crunching jagged shards of broken glass that covered every surface. A fog of white dust hung in the air. 'I've got to get out of here,' thought Brian Espe, hunkered down beneath a massive conference table on the fifth floor of the federal building moments after a car bomb ripped its guts out and peeled off the north wall. 'But I've got to be very careful.' Espe, 57, an Agriculture Department veterinarian, picked himself up gingerly from the rubble and looked around. He noticed that some USDA offices, like his conference room, had been turned upside down as if by a cyclone, but most of the fifth floor was simply obliterated: 'the north side of the building disappeared,' Espe said. 'I could walk through a wall and step into space.' Fortunately, he was on the south side, far from the explosion but still teetering on the edge of oblivion."

Pictures of the building taken a week later by FEMA

Pictures of the extent of the damage taken by FEMA

For each life that the bomb took that morning, it changed 100 others. 48 year old James Hargrave, who worked on the third floor in the Office of the Inspector General of the Department of Health and Human Services, told the *New York Times*, "I was on the phone and did not hear any explosion, just felt things falling on my head. And I really thought it was an earthquake or something similar. When I stood, I was completely free; it just kind of all fell around me. And I searched for the people in my office. The strange thing was, it was like I was the only person alive. There was no screaming, no moaning, no hissing from gas lines, none of the things you so normally see on a TV show. It was almost silent. I found most of the people in my office, and we dug them out. And there didn't seem to be anyone that was hurt severely, and our first inclination was to get out. And I said, 'Well, is anybody hurt?' And this other voice said: 'Yes, I'm hurt. Could you help me?' And we found this guy that was in our office, and we kind of start digging him out. And we ask him, 'Who are you?' And he said that he was from the seventh floor. ... We jerked them down, tied them into a knot, these huge curtains that went from ceiling to floor, and they kind of used it as a hammock and a rope at the same time. They kind of laid on it and kind of just scooted down the side of the building."

Hargrave then made a grim observation, the result of a detachment caused by a combination of shock and sorrow: "The only bad thing about this story, because all of our people are not hurt seriously, was the one young lady has an infant in the day-care center.... And when you get out, we had to actually -- the level we got out on the ground is the day-care playground. So we had to walk through that playground, and then we found out later that most of the babies and young children had died." In fact, some of the children in the center did survive and, seeing their teachers and friends dead around them, ran from the area looking for the only people they thought might be able to help them. Calvin Johnson, a janitor at an Oklahoma hotel, recalled, "I was coming out of the courthouse when I was thrown against the building wall. Initially I saw glass falling and two cars in the middle of the street, and I thought there had been a car wreck. Then I saw the smoke and realized what had happened. I ran toward the Federal building, a block away. I wasn't concerned about myself, because I was on my feet. I wanted to see if there was something I could do for someone else. There were people running past me, all bloody, and I saw a kid running along -- he was 2 or 3 years old, a little black kid. I think he thought I was his father. He was hollering: 'Dad! Dad!' I picked him up and carried him to the other side of the street, to the corner where the courthouse is. By this time, the streets were loaded with people running from every side. I don't have any idea how he is, or how his family is. I don't remember what he was wearing, and if somebody was to hand him to me now, I wouldn't know if it was him or not."

Fortunately, some parents were able to find their children, even in the minutes after the bombing. Ondre King worked across the street from the Murrah Federal Building and had a 2 year old daughter in the daycare center. The day after the attack, she said, "She was already outside by the time I got there. She was just drenched with blood. ... And there was a whole bunch of ambulances and police out there. And I seen all that black smoke, and it looked like there was a car on fire. And when we got to the hospital at like 9:30, then she started hollering and crying, because they started messing with her. And they had to sedate her to work with her. And I thought, 'Oh, my God, my baby's finger was blown off, and they had to sew it back on.' I think the glass, it hurt, because she got stitches all on the rim of her ears, and on the back of her ears. Then she got I don't know how many stitches on her thumb. That was cut pretty deep, on the left hand. And she has stitches on her left thigh. And she has a few scratches on her face and a few scratches on her cheek and on her back. Her back is pretty bruised. And she still has glass and stuff in her hair. I'm still picking glass and stuff out of my hair. I think they're kind of embedded in my scalp; I'm scared to scratch it."

While it was the children's injuries and deaths that were the most heart wrenching, most of those harmed that day were adults. Wanda Webster was 65 and worked for the Office of Native American Programs of the Department of Housing and Urban Development in the building. She told reporters, "The blast hit, and it threw me up against a wall, and another wall collapsed on top of me. It was like the end of the world when the blast hit, this tremendous noise and pressure against you. And I could see everything disintegrating. I had no sense of direction, but I dug myself out of the rubble. I don't know how long it took, I was so disoriented. But I was in a pocket; our ceiling didn't collapse. And when I finally did remove the rubble and stand up, there was nothing there. You didn't know where you were. There were two other workers and myself. We started crawling toward some light. But then we realized we were crawling toward the edge of the window that had blown out, and we turned around and were able to get to the only remaining staircase. And we walked out of the building."

Not everyone injured was trapped in the rubble. Auditor Richard Slay explained, "I arrived at just about 9 o'clock and walked…right over to the elevators, punched the 'up' button. … As soon as the doors opened, the air in the elevator shaft started whooshing out. There must have been little pebbles and dirt in the elevator shaft getting sucked up. It pelted my right hand and my right arm, where I was just wearing a button-down shirt -- I had it rolled up. The blast of air came first, and then the explosion. I immediately dropped to the ground and kind of turned away from the elevator shaft, because I felt certain that there would be a fireball coming out there. I didn't want to get blasted in the face. But the fireball never came. And the building just started sliding into the street. I could just hear it. And right above me, all around me, the first thing, the most immediate thing, was the redwood ceiling was falling. But it never touched me. And then some air ducts, that stuff was falling down. And other metal, aluminum-type sheeting stuff was falling. But none of it was hitting me. That was really miraculous. Then it all just kind of stopped, and it got very quiet."

Slay stood there for a few minutes before he reacted: "My first thought was, 'I'll just stay here until some rescue workers come.' Then I started smelling smoke, and that started changing my thinking a little bit. I had started calling out to see if there were survivors: 'Is anyone here?' I didn't get any responses. I heard some groans. It took a while to even start hearing groans…Then I noticed a white cloud moving in. I had never smelled that stuff before. It was acrid. I thought it must have been gas from the explosion…I started moving. I was walking over mounds of rubble. Then I heard a lady say, 'I think I have an exit here.' She opened a door. There was a lot of light coming in, but there was so much rubble I told her I didn't think we wanted to walk through all that mess. With the light, I could see the double doors to the loading dock. I said, 'Let's go this way.' Outside I looked east, and it was just a nightmare. The cars were on fire, and there were plumes of smoke everywhere. So we went west across the street to the Catholic rectory. By this time, the lady I was with just collapsed. She just crumpled to the ground."

Fire trucks, ambulances and other vehicles quickly arrived on the scene. Paramedic John Grifith remembered, "It's like they dumped it in with a dump truck. Imagine taking an office and putting it in a blender and turning it on. Everything was upside down — computers, keyboards." He told the story of one woman he was trying to rescue when the workers were ordered from the building due to fears of further collapse. The woman begged Grifith not to leave her. "I said, 'I don't want to, but they're making me.' I put myself in her place, and thought how terribly alone." When he got back to her 45 minutes later, "She kept asking over and over if we would ever get her out. I told her she was just having a bad hair day and they were going to dock her for laying down on the job." In the wake of the attacks, firefighter Mike Roberts told reporters, "We've been digging on this lady for the last hour. She's still alive. I gave her water. I said, 'We're going to get you out.' She said, 'Do you think you can?' I said, 'Yeah." Finally, five hours later, the woman was carried out. According to the article, "As she was loaded into the ambulance, a chaplain approached Grifith. Standing in the pouring rain with the shell of the federal building behind them, they closed their eyes, bowed their heads and prayed."

A news service article reported, "The blast occurred at the start of a work day, as parents dropped off their youngsters at the day-care center in the federal building. Before the smoke cleared, emergency worker Heather Taylor had put tags on the toes of at least 12 children. Assistant Fire Chief Jon Hansen described the first 30 minutes after the bombing as 'pure mayhem.' Streets were choked with walking wounded, emergency crews and well-meaning citizens. Some people, apparently driving near the federal building at the time of the blast, appeared to have been killed in their cars. Inside the federal building, survivors were screaming and crying, Hansen said, 'We're having to crawl over victims to try and reach the living, and often all we can do is hold their hand.' … By noon, the only sounds rescuers in the federal building could hear were made by other rescue workers, said Officer Adrian Neal of the Edmond Police Department. By 1:30 p.m., many medical personnel were sent home."

A picture of the Alfred P. Murrah Building after the attack

A picture of rescue workers receiving communion

A picture of rescue efforts taken on April 21

Pictures of search and rescue and salvage operations

Chapter 4: 75 Minutes Later

"Approximately 75 minutes later, about 75 miles north of Oklahoma City, the exact distance from Oklahoma City that you could drive in that time if you had been at the scene of the crime, the exact distance...you would reach between the time of the bombing and the time he was arrested if you were driving at normal speed limit. And on his clothing, an FBI chemist later found residue of explosives, undetonated explosives, not the kind of residue that would detonate in the course of the explosion but the kind of explosives you would have on your clothing if you had made the bomb.... And the T-shirt he was wearing virtually broadcast his intention. On its front was the image of Abraham Lincoln; and beneath the image was a phrase about tyrants, which is a phrase that John Wilkes Booth shouted in Ford's Theater to the audience when he murdered President Lincoln. And on the back of the T-shirt that McVeigh was wearing on that morning...was this phrase: It said, 'The tree of liberty must be refreshed from time to time with the blood of patriots and tyrants.' And above those words was the image of a tree...the tree on the T-shirt bears a depiction of droplets of scarlet-red blood." – Joseph Hartzler, prosecutor in the case against McVeigh

"I am sorry these people had to lose their lives. But that's the nature of the beast. It's understood going in what the human toll will be." – Timothy McVeigh

While people were responding to the explosion, McVeigh was driving down the highway, intent on making his escape. However, he had made a critical error, one that would ultimately bring him to justice. State Trooper Charles Hanger explained in his testimony, "I was northbound on the interstate in the left-hand lane when I came upon a vehicle which was a yellow 1977 Mercury Marquis, four-door. It had a primer spot on the left rear quarter panel. And I started around that vehicle in the left lane, it was in the right lane traveling north, I observed that it was not displaying a tag on the rear bumper. I slowed down, fell in behind the vehicle, got in the same lane it was in. Initiated my emergency lights and signaled for it to pull over. It began slowing down and pulling over to the east side of the roadway, the shoulder. ... We met behind his car. About 3 or 4 feet south of the left rear corner of his car and off to the west 3 or 4 feet. And I told him why I'd stopped him."

McVeigh was polite and cooperative, but in the next few moments, his situation evolved from being issued a traffic ticket, or maybe just a warning, to being arrested on a felony. Hanger noted, "As he was going to his right rear pocket to retrieve his billfold, he had on a blue windbreaker-type jacket that was just slightly zipped, and when he went to his pocket, it tightened this jacket up somewhat; and I could see a bulge under his left arm, and I thought that that was a weapon under his arm. I looked at the driver's license and looked at him. Then I instructed him to take both hands, unzip his jacket, and to very slowly move his jacket back. He took both hands, he unzipped his jacket, and started slowly pulling it back; and just as he started doing that, he said, 'I have a gun.' I grabbed for the bulge, and I said, 'Put your hands up and turn around.' ... I removed my pistol from my holster and stuck it to the back of his head. I instructed him to walk to the trunk of his automobile."

McVeigh had to have been aware by this time that he was now in deep trouble. Still, he remained polite and cooperative in every way possible. According to Hanger, "He said, 'My weapon is loaded.' I said, 'So is mine.' I instructed him to put his hands on the trunk and to spread his feet. ... I then pulled back the jacket, removed the pistol from the holster it was in, and threw it on the shoulder of the roadway. ... He informed me that he also had another clip and a pouch on his belt. ... He told me that he also had a knife on his belt. ... I then patted him down and handcuffed him. ... I took him to the right front passenger seat of my unit, placed him in there and seat-belted him in. ... I placed [the gun and the knife] in the trunk of my unit. Also checked the weapon to see if it was loaded. Removed the clip from the bottom of the weapon, then I checked the chamber of the weapon and removed a round from that chamber. ... I asked him if he wanted me to tow the car or leave it at the roadside. And I explained to him the difference, that if I impound the car, I'll make a inventory of it and list his property for his protection, and if he leaves it at the roadside, it will be left at his own risk. He said, "Just leave it."

As a result, McVeigh was charged with "Transporting a loaded firearm in a motor vehicle, unlawfully carrying a weapon, failure to display a current number plate, which is a tag, on a motor vehicle and failure to maintain proof of security, which is liability insurance." Later that day, as McVeigh sat in his holding cell, President Clinton spoke to the American people:

> "The bombing in Oklahoma City was an attack on innocent children and defenseless citizens. It was an act of cowardice, and it was evil. The United States will not tolerate it. And I will not allow the people of this country to be intimidated by evil cowards. I have met with our team, which we assembled to deal with this bombing. And I have determined to take the following steps to assure the strongest response to this situation:

> "First, I have deployed a crisis management team under the leadership of the FBI, working with the Department of Justice, the Bureau of Alcohol, Tobacco and Firearms, military and local authorities. We are sending the world's finest investigators to solve these murders.

> "Second, I have declared an emergency in Oklahoma City. And at my direction, James Lee Witt, the Director of the Federal Emergency Management Agency, is now on his way there to make sure we do everything we can to help the people of Oklahoma deal with the tragedy.

> "Third, we are taking every precaution to reassure and to protect people who work in or live near other Federal facilities.

"Let there be no room for doubt: We will find the people who did this. When we do, justice will be swift, certain, and severe. These people are killers, and they must be treated like killers. Finally, let me say that I ask all Americans tonight to pray—to pray for the people who have lost their lives, to pray for the families and the friends of the dead and the wounded, to pray for the people of Oklahoma City. May God's grace be with them. Meanwhile, we will be about our work."

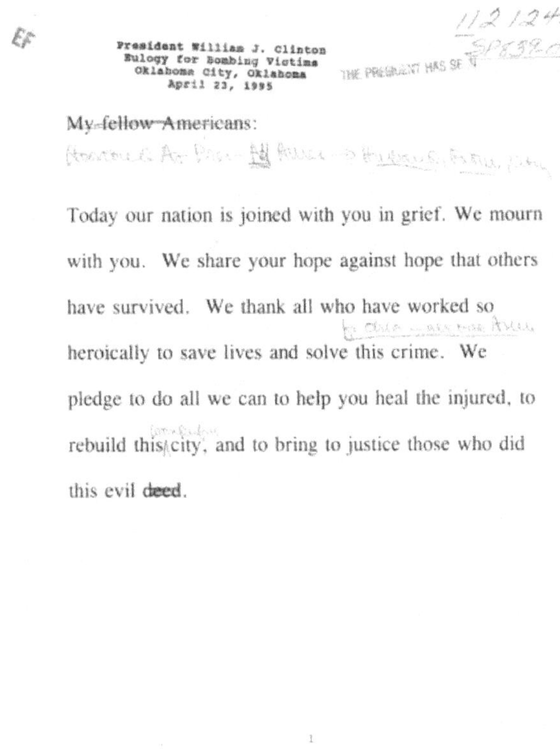

President William J. Clinton
Eulogy for Bombing Victims
Oklahoma City, Oklahoma
April 23, 1995

THE PRESIDENT HAS SEEN

My fellow Americans:

Today our nation is joined with you in grief. We mourn

with you. We share your hope against hope that others

have survived. We thank all who have worked so

heroically to save lives and solve this crime. We

pledge to do all we can to help you heal the injured, to

rebuild this city, and to bring to justice those who did

this evil deed.

A picture of Clinton's personal notes for his address on the bombing

Furthermore, Clinton wrote to Frank Keating, the Governor of Oklahoma, assuring him, "I have declared an emergency under the Robert T. Stafford Disaster Relief and Emergency Assistance Act (the Stafford Act) for the city of Oklahoma City in the State of Oklahoma due to the explosion at the Federal courthouse in Oklahoma City on April 19, 1995 in the State of Oklahoma. I have authorized Federal relief and emergency assistance in the affected area."

By this time, Trooper Hanger had become aware of two critical pieces of evidence. The first was something he overheard: "I had heard Mrs. Moritz [the woman booking McVeigh] ask him who he wanted to list as next of kin. And he didn't say anything. And I heard her ask that same question again. He still didn't say anything. So I…got up from the chair that I was sitting in at the computer and walked up to the booking counter. … And I said, 'Well, what about the address listed on the license?' I said, 'Who lives there?' … He said that was a place that he had stayed; it was a -- belonged to a brother of a friend that he was in the military with. … The last name was Nichols. At that particular time I couldn't remember what the first name was."

By this time, the police had circulated a sketch of a man they called "John Doe No. 1." The sketch was based on descriptions they had received from witnesses at the site. Ironically, one of his former co-workers had identified McVeigh as the suspect, and the police had issued a warrant for his arrest. When the federal authorities learned the man they were looking for was already in custody, they picked McVeigh up and transferred him to Tinker Air Force Base.

An FBI sketch of the suspect next to McVeigh's mugshot

That evening, Terry Nichols went to the police station in Herington and turned himself in and gave them permission to search his house. Shortly thereafter, Trooper Hanger discovered another critical piece of evidence: "On the morning of the 22d, which would be the next shift that I worked after completing my shift on the 19th, I'd went to work that day, and I made a search of the, visual search of the area of my car. I always look at the floorboards and the seats to see if anything that might have been left in there that could be used as a weapon. And while I was doing that, I looked in the right rear floorboard and there was a crumpled-up white business card laying in the floorboard. … It says, 'Paulsen's Military Supply.' [On the back] In big capital letters it says, 'Dave,' and then in parentheses, it says '(TNT @ $5 a stick. Need more.)' Below that is a telephone number that says, '708-288-0128.' Below that in printing it says, 'Call after 1

May see if I can get some more.'"

Chapter 5: This Terrible Crime

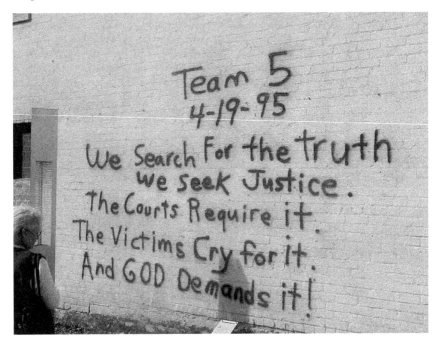

Graffiti left by Rescue Team 5 in remembrance of the victims

"Each of the crimes has various elements. The Judge at the end of the case will instruct you on those elements. It's our burden to prove each of the elements for each of the counts. We will meet that burden. We will make your job easy. We will present ample evidence to convince you beyond any reasonable doubt that Timothy McVeigh is responsible for this terrible crime. You will hear evidence in this case that McVeigh liked to consider himself a patriot, someone who could start the second American Revolution. The literature that was in his car when he was arrested included some that quoted statements from the founding fathers and other people who played a part in the American Revolution, people like Patrick Henry and Samuel Adams. McVeigh isolated and took these statements out of context, and he did that to justify his anti-government violence. Well, ladies and gentlemen, the statements of our forefathers can never be televised to justify warfare against innocent children. Our forefathers didn't fight British women and children. They fought other soldiers. They fought them face to face, hand to hand. They didn't plant bombs and run away wearing earplugs" – Joseph Hartzler, prosecutor in the case against McVeigh

"I knew I wanted this before it happened. I knew my objective was state-assisted suicide and when it happens, it's in your face. You just did something you're trying to say should be illegal for medical personnel." – Timothy McVeigh

On April 27, 1995, the United States District Court for the Western District of Oklahoma heard the evidence against McVeigh, and at the end of that proceeding, the U.S. Attorney concluded, "You have heard evidence, Your Honor, more than sufficient to establish that during and relation to a crime of violence the Defendant used and carried a destructive device that is a bomb. Therefore, the presumption applies and should be detained. ... Finally, Your Honor with respect to the safety of the community, the statute directs us to look at the nature of the offense and could not imagine a more heinous offense than this. The Defendant has shown a willingness to kill innocent children, law enforcement officers, and ordinary people going about their ordinary lives. No series of the conditions could reasonably assure his appearance or the safety of other persons in the community. For that reason, he should be detained." The next day, the United States Magistrate ordered McVeigh held without bail. Nichols, however, was not formally arrested until May 10.

A picture of McVeigh in custody

A picture of the Murrah Federal Building being demolished in May 1995

A few days after McVeigh's arraignment, on May 4, the search for bodies in the remains of the Murrah Federal Building ended. The next day, an Associated Press article reported that "firefighters found the remains of the last nine victims, Assistant Fire Chief Jon Hansen said. The grim discovery in the last 6- foot pile of unsearched rubble brought the death toll to 168 and came despite fears earlier in the week that some of the bodies would never be found. Among the sets of nearly two dozen remains uncovered on Thursday were those of the last three children unaccounted for in the April 19 terrorist bombing. With the search at an end after 17 days, families will be allowed to gather at the site for one last, private remembrance, possibly this weekend."

After this, all that was left for those grieving was to try to move on, whether it was through faith in some future reunion or a hope for justice in the present. On June 14, the federal government tightened its case on McVeigh and Nichols, but it eliminated the search for "John Doe No. 2," concluding that the person in question likely had nothing to do with the bombings.

The cases against McVeigh and Nichols got their next big boost when Michael and Lori Fortier agreed to testify against the men in exchange for leniency for Michael and immunity for Lori. Michael admitted, "Prior to April 1995, McVeigh told me about the plans that he and Terry

Nichols had to blow up the Federal Building in Oklahoma City, Oklahoma. I did not as soon as possible make known my knowledge of the McVeigh and Nichols plot to any judge or other persons in civil authority. When F.B.I. agents questioned me later, about two days after the bombing, and during the next three days, I lied about my knowledge and concealed information. For example, I falsely stated that I had no knowledge of plans to bomb the federal building. I also gave certain items that I had received from McVeigh, including a bag of ammonium nitrate fertilizer, to a neighbor of mine so the items would not be found by law enforcement officers in a search of my residence."

On August 11, 1995, the grand jury hearing the case against McVeigh and Nichols returned an indictment: "Beginning on or about September 13, 1994 and continuing thereafter until on or about April 19, 1995...TIMOTHY JAMES McVEIGH and TERRY LYNN NICHOLS...did knowingly, intentionally, willfully and maliciously conspire, combine and agree together and with others unknown to the Grand Jury to use a weapon of mass destruction, namely an explosive bomb placed in a truck (a "truck bomb"), against persons within the United States and against property that was owned and used by the United States...resulting in death, grievous bodily injury and destruction of the building...It was the object of the conspiracy to kill and injure innocent persons and to damage property of the United States...As intended by McVEIGH and NICHOLS, the truck bomb explosion resulted in death and personal injury and the destruction of the Alfred P. Murrah Federal Building, located within the Western District of Oklahoma."

On October 20, Attorney General Janet Reno announced that she had ordered the government's prosecutors to seek the death penalty if McVeigh and Nichols were convicted. McVeigh's lawyer, Stephen Jones, noted, "The news hardly comes as a surprise. The attorney general and the president announced they would seek the death penalty before they even knew who the defendants were. ... We will mount our attack on the obvious pre-judgment of the case." Of course, given the national mood and the fact that the case against McVeigh was solid, technicalities were all that Jones had to work with. On December 1, he persuaded the 10th Circuit Court of Appeals to remove Judge Wayne Alley of Oklahoma and put the case under the jurisdiction of Judge Richard Matsch in Denver. Nearly three months later, Matsch ordered the trial itself moved to Denver, since he felt that the people of Oklahoma were too prejudiced to offer McVeigh a fair trial. In October 1996, Matsch ordered that McVeigh and Nichols be tried separately, and that McVeigh be tried first. This move may very well have saved Nichols' life.

On February 28, 1997, the public and the courts were shocked when the *Dallas Morning News* published an article with allegedly obtained documents that quoted McVeigh as confessing to the bombing. Particularly shocking was a quote from someone present at a July 1995 interview. When asked why he didn't just bomb the building at night, the staffer reported, "McVeigh looked directly into my eyes and told me, 'That would not have gotten the point across to the government. We needed a body count to make our point.'" The article also reported, "McVeigh again insisted that he was the one who drove the Ryder truck. ... McVeigh stated that James Nichols had no knowledge about the bombing as far as he knew, but that he didn't know what Terry Nichols might have told brother James."

For a time, it appeared as though these leaked remarks could derail the government's plans for the case, but the process went forward and jury selection began on March 31, 1997. The prosecution then made its opening statements, during which Joseph Hartzler referenced an envelope Officer Hanger had found in McVeigh's car the day he stopped him. "Enclosed in that envelope were slips of paper bearing statements that McVeigh had clipped from books and newspapers. And one of them was a quotation that -- from a book that McVeigh had copied. ...and he highlighted this -- 'The real value of our attacks today lies in the psychological impact, not in the immediate casualties.' Another slip of paper...reads, in part, 'When the government fears the people, there is liberty.' ... And hand-printed beneath those printed words, in McVeigh's handwriting, are the words...'Maybe now there will be liberty.' These documents are virtually a manifesto declaring McVeigh's intention. Everyone in this great nation has a right to think and believe, speak whatever they want. We are not prosecuting McVeigh because we don't like his thoughts or his beliefs or even his speech; we're prosecuting him because his hatred boiled into violence, and his violence took the lives of innocent men and women and children. And the reason we'll introduce evidence of his thoughts, as disclosed by those writings and others, is because they reveal his premeditation and his intent, and intent is an element of the crime that we must prove."

In response, the defense asserted, "I believe that when you see the evidence in this case, you will conclude that the investigation of the Alfred P. Murrah Building lasted about two weeks. The investigation to build the case against Timothy McVeigh lasted about two years. But within 72 hours after suspicion first centered on Mr. McVeigh. We will prove to you that even then, the Government knew, the FBI agents in the case, that the pieces of the puzzle were not coming together; that there was something terribly wrong, something missing. And as Paul Harvey says, our evidence will be the rest of the story."

Over the next month, the prosecution presented 137 witnesses, all of whom offered evidence against McVeigh. Then the defense took over, spending less than a week calling 25 witnesses. The two sides made their closing arguments on May 29 and the case was turned over to the jury. After just a few days of deliberation, they found McVeigh guilty on June 2 on all 11 counts against him. In thanking them for their service, the judge observed, "Members of the jury, you have determined by your verdict that the evidence established the guilt of Timothy McVeigh on these charges beyond a reasonable doubt of crimes for which death is a possible punishment. Whether Mr. McVeigh should be put to death for these crimes is a question to be answered by the jury serving as the conscience of the community. Although Congress has given this responsibility exclusively to the jury, the applicable statute and the Constitution command that you must exercise your discretion by following a specific procedure and give careful and thoughtful consideration to information characterized as 'aggravating and mitigating factors' to be presented now in a court hearing that is in a sense an extension or continuation of the trial...."

After more than a week of arguments for and against executing McVeigh, the jury decided unanimously on June 13, 1997 to sentence him to death. The judge announced, "Timothy James McVeigh, pursuant to the jury verdict returned on June 2, 1997, finding you guilty on all 11 counts of the indictment, the defendant is adjudged guilty of each of the following offenses: A conspiracy to use a weapon of mass destruction as charged in Count One, the use of a weapon of mass destruction as charged in Count Two, destruction by explosive as charged in Count Three, and first degree murder as charged in Counts Four through Eleven. Pursuant to the Federal Death Penalty Act of 1994, appearing in 18 United States Code Sections 3591 to 3596 and the special findings of the jury returned on June 13, 1997, and the jury's unanimous vote recommending that the defendant shall be sentenced to death, it is the judgment of the Court that the defendant, Timothy James McVeigh, is sentenced to death on each of the 11 counts of the indictment."

A picture of the supermax prison in Colorado where McVeigh was incarcerated alongside the Unabomber and Ramzi Yousef on "Bomber's Row"

While McVeigh's attorneys continued to appeal his conviction and the sentence, Terry Nichols was tried during the fall of 1997 and convicted on of most of the counts against him on December 23. However, he was found "not guilty" of actually using a weapon of mass destruction, and when the jury deliberated on his sentence, they could not agree on the death penalty. The *Washington Post* reported, "There was no evidence that Nichols had rented the Ryder truck used to carry the bomb to Oklahoma City, and there was no one who could positively identify him as the purchaser of the two tons of ammonium nitrate, the major component in the bomb. Most problematic for the government was the compelling fact that

Nichols was at home in Kansas when McVeigh detonated the truck." Therefore, Nichols was sentenced on June 4, 1998 to life without parole. By this time, Michael Fortier had already began serving a 12 year sentence for his role in the conspiracy.

Each of McVeigh's appeals failed, and the Supreme Court ultimately refused to hear his case. On July 13, 1999 he was moved to the federal penitentiary in Terre Haute, Indiana to await execution. CBS reporter Ed Bradley interviewed him there on March 12, 2000 and later said, "Well, his rationalization, is because of the policies of this government. And it keys on what happened at Waco, and I guess Ruby Ridge, and I mean that is what he thinks is wrong with this government. And that this government is working against people he would regard as patriots. I'm not [surprised he wants to die]. I think that -- I think that he feels that this is the best way for him to go. I read something of what he planned to say -- at least, what he has said he plans to say before he dies in his last words, that he is the captain of his ship. He is the captain of his fate. And in that sense, in that he has said, I'm going to waive all my appeals, kill me -- in that sense he feels that he is deciding his fate."

A picture of the penitentiary in Terre Haute

While at the penitentiary in Terre Haute, McVeigh wrote a letter that discussed the bombing, as well as an attempt to justify his actions:

"The administration has said that Iraq has no right to stockpile chemical or biological weapons ("weapons of mass destruction") — mainly because they have used them in the past.

"Well, if that's the standard by which these matters are decided, then the U.S. is the nation that set the precedent. The U.S. has stockpiled these same weapons (and more) for over 40 years. The U.S. claims this was done for deterrent purposes during its 'Cold War' with the Soviet Union. Why, then, it is invalid for Iraq to claim the same reason (deterrence) with respect to Iraq's (real) war with, and the continued threat of, its neighbor Iran?

"The administration claims that Iraq has used these weapons in the past. We've all seen the pictures that show a Kurdish woman and child frozen in death from the use of chemical weapons. But, have you ever seen those pictures juxtaposed next to pictures from Hiroshima or Nagasaki?

"I suggest that one study the histories of World War I, World War II and other 'regional conflicts' that the U.S. has been involved in to familiarize themselves with the use of "weapons of mass destruction."

Remember Dresden? How about Hanoi? Tripoli? Baghdad? What about the big ones — Hiroshima and Nagasaki? (At these two locations, the U.S. killed at least 150,000 non-combatants — mostly women and children — in the blink of an eye. Thousands more took hours, days, weeks or months to die).

"If Saddam is such a demon, and people are calling for war crimes charges and trials against him and his nation, why do we not hear the same cry for blood directed at those responsible for even greater amounts of 'mass destruction' — like those responsible and involved in dropping bombs on the cities mentioned above?

"The truth is, the U.S. has set the standard when it comes to the stockpiling and use of weapons of mass destruction...

"Hypocrisy when it comes to the death of children? In Oklahoma City, it was family convenience that explained the presence of a day-care center placed between street level and the law enforcement agencies which occupied the upper floors of the building. Yet, when discussion shifts to Iraq, any day-care center in a government building instantly becomes 'a shield.' Think about it.

"When considering morality and 'mens rea', in light of these facts, I ask: Who are the true barbarians? ...

"I find it ironic, to say the least, that one of the aircraft used to drop such a bomb on Iraq is dubbed 'The Spirit of Oklahoma.' This leads me to a final, and unspoken, moral hypocrisy regarding the use of weapons of mass destruction.

"When a U.S. plane or cruise missile is used to bring destruction to a foreign people, this nation rewards the bombers with applause and praise. What a convenient way to absolve these killers of any responsibility for the destruction they leave in their wake.

"Unfortunately, the morality of killing is not so superficial. The truth is, the use of a truck, a plane or a missile for the delivery of a weapon of mass destruction does not alter the nature of the act itself.

"These are weapons of mass destruction — and the method of delivery matters little to those on the receiving end of such weapons.

"Whether you wish to admit it or not, when you approve, morally, of the bombing of foreign targets by the U.S. military, you are approving of acts morally equivalent to the bombing in Oklahoma City..."

On January 16, 2001, McVeigh announced that he was dropping the rest of his appeals, and the court set his execution date for four months later. Then, suddenly, there was a twist in the case when new documents came to light that the Justice Department admitted had not been shared previously with the defense. The new Attorney General, John Ashcroft, insisted that the execution be postponed for one month so that the defense could have a chance to review the more than 4,000 pages of documents.

On June 1, McVeigh announced that he had changed his mind and would in fact continue the appeals process, but a week later, having heard from all sides, the appeals court again denied McVeigh's stay. Before his sentence was carried out, he ruminated on the idea of an afterlife and claimed, "If there is a hell, then I'll be in good company with a lot of fighter pilots who also had to bomb innocents to win the war."

Timothy McVeigh was executed by lethal injection on June 11, 2001. For his last words, he chose the poem "Invictus" by the Victorian poet William Earnest Henley.

"Out of the night that covers me,
Black as the pit from pole to pole,
I thank whatever gods may be
For my unconquerable soul.

"In the fell clutch of circumstance
I have not winced nor cried aloud.
Under the bludgeonings of chance
My head is bloody, but unbowed.

"Beyond this place of wrath and tears
Looms but the Horror of the shade,
And yet the menace of the years

Finds, and shall find me, unafraid.

"It matters not how strait the gate,
How charged with punishments the scroll,
I am the master of my fate:
I am the captain of my soul."

Family members of the victims were on hand to witness McVeigh's execution, but it didn't necessarily bring closure, with more than one bemoaning the fact that McVeigh didn't seem the least bit remorseful. In reference to the fact McVeigh declined to give a final statement just before his execution, Jay Sawyer complained, "Without saying a word, he got the final word." Larry Whicher, who lost his brother, said McVeigh had "a totally expressionless, blank stare. He had a look of defiance and that if he could, he'd do it all over again." Disturbingly, McVeigh went so far as to ask that his remains be located at the site of the memorial for the bombing, an act even he ultimately deemed "too vengeful, too raw, too cold."

McVeigh was gone, but victims were still upset that Nichols wasn't. Disappointed that the jury did not give Nichols the death penalty, the State of Oklahoma successfully appealed to try him on 161 counts of first degree murder. The trial took place in the spring of 2004 and led to more than 150 witnesses being called. In the end, Nichols was found guilty, but the jury in Oklahoma could not agree on a death sentence. CNN reported, "Nichols sat straight in his chair Friday as the jury foreman handed a note to Taylor that said, 'We will not be able to reach a unanimous verdict.' 'Sometimes this is how trials end up,' [Judge Steven] Taylor said. Nichols' mother, sister and ex-wife sat in the front row on one side of the courtroom, while bombing victims and their families sat on the other side of the aisle. 'This is unbelievable to me,' said the relative of one of the bombing victims, pointing to all the evidence presented by prosecutors. The jury returned to the courtroom twice Friday so its foreman could tell the judge the panel appeared hopelessly divided. The second time, Taylor told the jurors they could resume their talks or give up. After deliberating another hour, jurors returned to the courtroom with their final decision. ... 'Each and every one of these people died so [Nichols and McVeigh] could make a political statement,' prosecutor Sandra Elliott told the jury Wednesday in her closing arguments. Defense lawyers described Nichols as the pawn of a 'dominant, manipulative and controlling' McVeigh. The prosecution and defense called 87 witnesses over five days of testimony in the penalty phase of the trial, many of them relatives still grieving over their losses nine years ago. Nichols' attorney, Creekmore Wallace, urged jurors not to be swayed by 'that flood of tears, that flood of pain' related by victims who testified."

With nothing else he could do, Judge Taylor used his own authority to add 160 more life sentences to the one Nichols already had.

Online Resources

Other 20th century history titles by Charles River Editors

Other titles about Timothy McVeigh on Amazon

Other books about The Unabomber on Amazon

Bibliography

Chase, Alston. *Harvard and the Unabomber: The Education of an American Terrorist.* Norton, 2003.

City of Oklahoma City Document Management (1996). Final Report: Alfred P. Murrah Federal Building Bombing April 19, 1995. Stillwater, OK: Department of Central Services Central Printing Division.

Giordano, Geraldine (2003). The Oklahoma City Bombing. New York: The Rosen Publishing Group, Inc.

Hoffman, David (1998). The Oklahoma City Bombing and the Politics of Terror. Feral House.

Kaczynski, Theodore. *Technological Slavery.* Feral House, 2010.

Kaczynski, David. *Every Last Tie: The Story of the Unabomber and His Family.* Duke University Press. 2016

Key, Charles, State Representative (2001). The Final Report of the Bombing of the Alfred P. Murrah Building. Oklahoma City, Oklahoma: The Oklahoma Bombing Investigation Committee.

Michel, Lou; Dan Herbeck (2001). American Terrorist: Timothy McVeigh & The Oklahoma City Bombing. New York: Regan Books.

Oklahoma Today (2005). 9:02 am, April 19, 1995: The Official Record of the Oklahoma City Bombing. Oklahoma City: Oklahoma Today.

Serano, Richard A. (1998). One of Ours: Timothy McVeigh and the Oklahoma City Bombing. New York: W. W. Norton & Company.

Sherrow, Victoria (1998). The Oklahoma City Bombing: Terror in the Heartland. Springfield, N.J.: Enslow Publishers.

CPSIA information can be obtained
at www.ICGtesting.com
Printed in the USA
BVHW041623250420
578459BV00011B/1690